Matthew Bazell is a native North Londoner. Born in Euston in 1977, he is a lifelong supporter of Arsenal FC and also follows Darlington FC and Millwall FC on the side. *Theatre of Silence* is his second book about football. His previous book, *Invasion and Deportation*, was published in 2000.

Rod Liddle was born in South London and is a lifelong supporter of Millwall FC. He is a respected and controversial figure in British journalism. He has edited the award winning *Today* programme on BBC Radio 4, presented documentaries for Channel 4, has had a column in *The Guardian* and edited *The Spectator*. He currently has a weekly column in *The Sunday Times*.

www.myspace.com/matthewbazell

The author recommends the reader to access the Football Supporters Federation website.

www.fsf.org.uk

THEATRE OF SILENCE

The lost soul of football

Matthew Bazell

THEATRE OF SILENCE
The lost soul of football

Pegasus

PEGASUS PAPERBACK

© Copyright 2008
Matthew Bazell

A CIP catalogue record for this title is
available from the British Library.

ISBN 978 1 903490 32 7

Pegasus is an imprint of
Pegasus Elliot MacKenzie Publishers Ltd.
www.pegasuspublishers.com

First Published in 2008

Pegasus
Sheraton House Castle Park
Cambridge CB3 0AX England

Printed & Bound in Great Britain

Dedications

Theatre of Silence is dedicated to the memory of Louis
Calcagni and Richard Bazell.

A special thanks to...

Catherine Bazell, Rod Liddle, Tim Bazell, Katie Bazell, Ben Bazell, Dave Hooke, Jamie Mash, Marc Cohen, Gerry Fagbemi, Penny Bazell, Mel Prescott, Max Lowe, Mike Slicker, Will Moss, Tom Youlden, Carol Youlden, Margaretta Calcagni, Grant Jenkins, Paulo Vignali, Ant McGinley, Tim Watson, Chris Nicholson, Darren Stockdale, Alex Mabon, Anna Greenway, Petros Petrou, Fanos Charalambous, Kevin Proctor, Jon Ewart, Wigan Athletic ticket office, Kim Frost, Shakirah Mustafa, Neg Dupree, Lee Fernandes, Nikki Kenny, Tina Hannon, Mark Hannon, Stephen Pickup, John Finnegan, Andrew Evangelou, Marcus Evangelou, Alex Keazor, Marco Aleni, Luca Pugliese, Cvetanka Atanasova, Mirjana Mihajlevic, Thomas Tsui.

Foreword by Rod Liddle

I first met Matt in the interminable queue for a drink at half time during one of Millwall's witless and desolating home defeats last year. Against Northampton, maybe, or Brighton. I'd been sitting in my usual seat in the west upper stand, enduring the usual misery, the ball lumped into the seats every fifteen seconds, our forward line as mobile and deft as a bunch of fucking Victorian wardrobes and me, freezing, all the while yearning for a drink. Should I leave my seat two minutes before half-time (or "the interval" as my Chelsea-supporting media friends call it), so that I can be served before full-time? But what if something happens, on the pitch? What if we score? So I sit there and wait until the bitter end, under a ludicrous, hopeless, delusion and finally get my pint of gassy piss just as the players come out for the second half. Nothing happened in that final two minutes. Maybe someone kicked someone else, or took a throw in, but that's about it. Stewards won't let me take the pint back to my seat in case I try to ram the plastic glass into the opposing full-back's eyeball. Can't drink alcohol in your seat, mate. Can't smoke any more. Can't call the ref a blind cunt. Nothing to alleviate the harrowing boredom. It was nil one at half time. Nil one is what it stayed. It's always nil one; nil one is a sort of given, at the Den.

I mention all this stuff, the, uh, downbeat side of watching Millwall so that you can appreciate how bizarre it was to meet Matt. You see, I have to go to Millwall: I've been supporting them for forty years or so and, as the Irishman sung, it's too late to stop now. Millwall are my team and it doesn't really make any difference if they're playing in the Premiership or the Southern Counties Doug and Dinsdale Pirhana Loan Shark League. I don't really have a choice in the issue: it's ingrained. But Matt came up and introduced himself to me as an Arsenal fan, a gooner – and the shock of hearing this, of meeting someone who *didn't have to be there but had chosen to come of his own free will* so disarmed me that I failed to do what Millwall supporters are meant to do when approached in their own ground by an oppo fan, and stab him or something. And as I listened to his story it struck me that I was pretty lucky, all things considered. I had it easy. There's always someone worse off than you, isn't there?

Matt's story – which I had related to me first while we queued for a drink and later, at subsequent Millwall games where we lost nil-one to someone shit – was basically an explanation as to why he was there. Why he preferred the lumpen dross I have to watch every week to the gilded, be-jewelled beauty of his own side, Arsenal. It began with a statement which made me think he was mentally ill: it's more fun at Millwall, he said. Where's the fucking fun, exactly, I wondered, a little mordantly? It's not much fun for me and still less for the players, to judge from the unfamiliarity and caution with which they address the ball. But it transpired that his point was that his team, Arsenal – and indeed the whole fabric of his chosen spectator sport, football – had changed beyond recognition. He had been left behind, somehow. It wasn't simply that he couldn't afford to go very often to the beautiful Emirates Stadium on account of the extortionate ticket prices. Nor simply that once there he would be sitting among people who remained silent throughout the game not because they were in awe of the football but because they went so irregularly – for the same reasons as Matt - that they didn't know the words to any of the songs. For Highbury Library, now read Emirates Morgue. It was something more atavistic and elemental; the remoteness of the players from the fans, for a start. Hired mercenaries possessed of no loyalty except to their careers and their bank balances. Possessed of no connectivity to the local area. Distant from the fans not merely financially, but not even speaking the same language – either metaphorically or indeed literally. (Remember the European Champions League tie between Arsenal and Bayern Munich a few seasons back? I remember cheering for Munich because, in Owen Hargreaves, they had the only British player on the pitch. And even Hargreaves only just sneaks below the bar…) If you're cheering for Arsenal – or Chelsea, Spurs, Manchester United, Liverpool etc – under those circumstances, what exactly is it that you're cheering *for?* The successful accumulation of money? That your club, either through the dubious benevolence of some strange Russki, or through the sale of replica shirts in Thailand, has made enough money to buy some French speaking bloke from the Cote D'Ivoire, who'll stay and kiss the badge for a couple of seasons until a more propitious offer crops up somewhere else? What's to cheer, if you're an old North Banker, or a Holte Ender, or from the Shed; just a name, an old agglomeration of vowels and consonants. A franchise. Chelsea, Arsenal, Villa, Burger king, Starbucks, Halliburton. Or maybe you're cheering a distant memory, of how it used to be.

Of course, you may find it difficult to get tickets for your club even if you can occasionally afford to do so, because there are a lot of new fans around. These are the people who have swallowed whole the New Football concept; football as a sort of lifestyle choice; yeah, of course, I was at the game on Saturday, won again, think they'll do it this year. The careful and considered acquisition of vicarious success. These new people, converts perhaps from the 1996 European Championship when football, oddly enough, didn't quite come home, do not wish to buy into torment, longeurs and misery. Why should they? Possessing no real attachment to the clubs they now claim to support, they are instead buying the human right to be uplifted by victory every week. And only victory every week will do. Did you see how many people turned up to Chelsea's Champion's League game against Rosenborg following a "mediocre" start to the season (third place! Oh, the ignominy!) and a bruising draw against Blackburn Rovers? Some 25,000, that's all – round about what Notts Forest and Sheffield Wednesday get for their Division One or Championship league games, week in week out. And that's the other point; these new converts to New Football have a commitment to their clubs which is as fragile and tenuous as the surface tension of water, a skin so thin that it will break at the slightest disturbing current. A fairly famous mate of mine in the media decided a few years ago that he "ought" to support a football team and alighted upon – hey, guess what, kids – Chelsea. It was rather like choosing between Conran and Heals for a sofa. I bet he wasn't there for the Rosenborg game. Even a hint at the withdrawal of success and these new fans will melt away into the night. Fair enough, I suppose, that's their choice; I don't hate these people, I don't want them *killed.* But they have wrought an enormous change on the game I love and it has not been for the better.

Chewing gum doesn't lose its flavour no matter how long you have it in your mouth. What happens is your taste buds become bored of the flavour and begin to ignore it, so it tastes of nothing even though really the same sugars are being released by the gum. So it is with winning football games. Begin every season expecting to lose two or three games and soon enough a home victory over Fulham or Wigan is so boring as to become unpalatable. A few seasons back, Millwall were relegated from the Championship in a season as dire and dispiriting as any I can remember in 40 years. Every game brought a new humiliation, another crushing of the soul. Then, one cold night in early winter, we played Norwich City, Darren Huckerby and all, and – quite unjustly – won the game one-nil. I'm not kidding: we were out all night in Bermondsey celebrating, me and my friends - utterly euphoric. If there is anything to be gained vicariously from football it is this sense of a shared ordeal, of a community suffering travails but still being there and, on those wonderful occasions, sharing the delight in an unlikely victory. Can you imagine the New Football converts buying into THAT sentimental rubbish?

Football has been tidied up, its edges smoothed down, its nastinesses outlawed. I suppose in many ways it is a more socially inclusive activity than it once was; women quite like it, these days, and gay people too, at Crystal Palace and Charlton. We see some magnificent football on our televisions – but we also see the empty terraces, and hear the bemused silences. Michel Platini blames the "malign" influence of money for creating a two tier system of haves and have nots. He's right, I suppose, but Matt has made me wonder who really are the "haves" in this equation. Those who still have their clubs, with a fan base rooted in the geographical area, who can afford to attend their matches, whose players earn scarcely more than they do and on occasion show a vestige of commitment – or the others, the ones who win everything.

Chapters

Prologue

Managing Director
Arsenal Football Club
Emirates Stadium
75 Drayton Park
London N5 1BU

Dear Managing Director,

Please find enclosed my current silver membership card. Feel free to cross my name off the list for the following season and save the club the price of a second class stamp. I'd hate for you guys to waste twenty-three pence, because we all have to work hard to make the club as profitable as possible, and I'm just trying to do my bit. You see the other day, I realised that the last time I actually used this membership card to buy a ticket from the club was way back in winter 2004.

That was when I decided that I'd finally had enough of being treated like a gullible customer who has unconditional loyalty no matter how badly they are treated. The good news is that there are plenty of others on the waiting list for one of these silver membership cards and I'm sure that you will have no problem with replacing my custom. However, the bad news is that one day thousands of others will wake up and send you a similar kind of letter including their 'valuable' membership cards or season tickets. At this moment it doesn't seem like anything to be too concerned about: but give it time. All I will say is that if times get hard and the attendance comes down; please don't come back to the likes of me to give the club support, because we'll treat you with the same amount of respect that you currently give to us.

You've marketed football to a new breed of consumer, therefore when things start to get tough; they are the ones you should demand loyalty from. Good luck, because you might need it.

A lot of fans will be surprised that I'm prepared to give up something so valuable as my silver membership. Something that is in such demand and wanted by so many thousands of others. But in reality it's just a piece of plastic (costing £26 a year) which gives me the right to apply for a match ticket. Next time I go to a restaurant maybe I should pay £26 to have a look at the menu? Of course as a silver member I appreciate the fact that I'm better off than a red member who pays £26 a year for the right to apply for a ticket only on the occasions when the tickets have not all been purchased by silver members. Yep, you guys are geniuses! I remember when the silver membership cards first came into effect, members got £1 off for every ticket purchased. That soon went and I can see why, as there's no way you can let us greedy bastards get away with so much as £1 a game.

Leaving Highbury was a difficult decision, but I could understand why any club would want to leave a 38,000 stadium for one that holds 60,000. In my naivety, I believed that a bigger capacity stadium would have allowed more of us to gain entry to the games at a more reasonable price. Not exactly a radical idea. Instead, the whole project was part of one big corporate money-making plan that has ripped to shreds the identity and heart of a football club. Watch out Arsenal, because if I ever become a billionaire I'm buying the club outright and the first thing I'm going to do is sack the board. Okay this is unlikely to happen! But just in case it does, I'm giving you plenty of warning. I'm currently checking for oil in the Finsbury Park area. After lowering ticket prices the next thing I'd do is pay off your friends at Emirates Airlines and rename the ground 'The Arsenal Stadium'. I know it's a bit controversial to name a football stadium after a football club or area these days, but for some reason I thought the name seemed to fit.

It's sad for me to give up my membership, because I've been a club member at Arsenal in some capacity every year since 1986. But at this moment in time I've never felt so detached from the club and from football in general. I certainly don't see myself as the kind of consumer that you hold in your plans, and I can no longer continue giving you my money.

Kind regards
Matthew Bazell

P.S. Good luck in the Deloitte money league in the coming years. I hear we stand a good chance.

Chapter 1
"It's all gone quiet..."

"For as much as there is a great noise in the city caused by the hustling over large balls from which many evils might arise, which God forbid we commend, and forbid such a game to be used in the city in the future."

Edward II – 1314

On the 15th August 1987 my dad, brother and I were having a kick-about in Finsbury Park, North London, just a quarter of a mile from the old Arsenal stadium, Highbury. I was ten years old at that time and had only been to Highbury a few times. This was the opening day of the 1987-88 season. Liverpool were in town and Arsenal under George Graham were a young team on the way up after a decade of mediocrity.

The crowd was massive that day, 54,703. Only 5,397 short of Arsenal's current ground capacity at the new Emirates Airlines Stadium. The pictures from the TV and newspapers the next day would show Highbury so full that some fans had managed to climb on top of the roof of the old North Bank to gain the best view in the house. Images dramatic enough to give today's health and safety fanatics a fatal heart attack. I wasn't in the stadium that day, but I still felt an experience of live football that I've always remembered. The noise of the crowd that day was theatre alone. The roars from the North Bank and Clock End could be felt in the fields of Finsbury Park and powered over the noise pollution of the Seven Sisters Road. Loud enough for the fields to have felt like the Highbury pitch itself. Although I wasn't inside the stadium I was in a good mood because one almighty roar told me that Arsenal had won the game 1-0. So you can imagine I was shocked to find out that we had actually lost the game 2-1! Liverpool would go on to win the title quite convincingly that season, losing only two games on the way. The noise that day was frightening. But it was great and it was seductive.

Nineteen years later, and midway into the 2005-06 season, I was at Highbury to watch Arsenal play Cardiff City in the FA Cup third round. Formerly a regular, my trips to Highbury had become a rarity and the Cardiff game would only be the second time I had been to the old stadium in its final season. My friend was late, and I was left waiting outside the stadium for him to arrive. A cheer went up, indicating that a goal had been scored. A cheer not seemingly loud enough to be that of the home crowd so I assumed that the 6,000 Cardiff fans were celebrating an early 1-0 lead. So I was delighted to hear the PA announcer declare that Robert Pires had put Arsenal into the lead.

Whilst standing outside Highbury I realised that if I was none the wiser I would have no idea that there was a football match going on inside being watched by 38,000 people. Then again, I might have started to wonder why there was horse manure all over Avenell Road and hot dog and burger stands on every corner. My friend arrived within about fifteen minutes of kick-off and we soon made our way inside the ground. When you arrive late at football matches nowadays, it can feel like you're a latecomer to the theatre or the cinema. The row of people that you ask to get up from their seats look unhappy to have been disturbed during the performance. Once in my seat, I noticed two fans a couple of rows in front of me having a conversation about the game. They were virtually whispering and it didn't sound anything more than a typical discussion on how the game was going. So why were they whispering? Perhaps because the modern football crowd is so quiet that they didn't want the surrounding fans overhearing their conversation. It was so quiet that you could have heard a pin drop. In fact at one point someone did actually drop a pin and the whole

North Bank jumped and turned around. In the first half, one nearby fan stood up and shouted out "For fuck's sake make some noise" before a steward told him to sit back down. Arsenal went 2-0 up early in the first half and the game was effectively over. I looked around me and started to analyse the faces of some of the 38,000 people who populated the football ground I used to consider a second home, and who now populate Arsenal's new stadium. I'm no psychiatrist but I felt I had as much expertise to judge a football crowd as any Freudian or Jungian.

Despite the propaganda that football is now a more suitable environment for children, the average age of the modern day supporter is forty-three years of age, and this was certainly reflected in the crowd that I analysed. In this crowd there were virtually no kids, no groups of teenagers, and not many old people either. This crowd was white, middle class and looked decidedly forty-three years old! The men and women around me had one dominant expression – a look of lethargy and detachment, to the point of boredom. It brought me to the conclusion that many people who do attend football today do so out of status and habit, rather than any genuine passion or sense of enjoyment. It's a pastime that they've chosen to be a part of their life, and to their credit they dedicate a lot of time and money towards this pastime. However the expressions on their faces forced me to question whether or not their time and money would be better spent elsewhere. It certainly reassured me that my decision not to be part of that world anymore on a full-time basis was the correct one. No one seems to smile at football any more, or even look like they're enjoying themselves. When did it all become so serious?

Sitting in such a quiet atmosphere among nearly 40,000 people is a very disconcerting experience. It's a claustrophobic feeling of emptiness and non-belonging. This environment is the theatre of silence. A theatre where the audience applauds in the right places, stands up when they're supposed to, and whispers so as not to disturb anyone else. They're spectators watching a performance, rather than being part of the performance. They've not realised that crowd participation is also a vital part of the entertainment. It bothers me that this type of fan makes up a football crowd these days, but, of course these people have every right to be there. They have every right to follow their team, which I don't doubt they really do care for, and I have no right telling other people how to behave at a football match. If they choose to watch a game in passive silence, then that's up to them and there's nothing wrong with that. Sometimes I like to sit back and watch a game of football quietly, especially if I attend a match as a neutral. But my concern is the people who are left on the outside looking in, the ones that have been replaced by the new affluent consumer. The thousands of fans who would create that passion from the stands, but who are now so isolated from the modern game that they will continue to remain on the outside, unless there is a change.

As visitors to Highbury for the FA Cup third round, Cardiff fans brought with them one of the worst reputations for football violence in the country. The reputation is well deserved and it was clear that there was no shortage of Soul Crew (Cardiff's hooligan firm) in North London on the day of the game. After the match a 300 strong mob of Arsenal's hooligan firm 'The Herd' made their way up the Blackstock Road en route to find the Soul Crew.

Now, of course, I don't condone hooliganism. Of all the things in this world to fight for, to fight for football seems like wasted energy. Hooliganism caused English clubs to be banned throughout Europe for five years from 1985, and is also the main reason that steel fences were put up in stadiums that ended ultimately with the deaths of ninety-six Liverpool fans at Hillsborough. Yet the sight of this Arsenal mob sat well with me just for one reason, and that was the expressions on the faces of the new breed of fan in the area who were walking towards Highbury and Islington tube station. They'd never seen this at Arsenal before, and most of them would have been under the impression that Arsenal do not and never have had a hooligan firm. But they knew that this mob must have been Arsenal and not Cardiff, on account of the accents. The confusion on people's faces interested me because the sight of this 300 strong mean-looking firm didn't fit in with their modern commercial ideal of football. This sight was a throwback to the 1980s, the so-called dark days of football. With the hooligans on one side and the new breed of consumer on the other, there was a contrast between two cultures who have each been responsible in their own way for "dark days of football". Dark days so different in application, but both in their own extreme way pushing out ordinary supporters.

The dark days in football are still here, but the pendulum has swung from one extreme to the other. The game of the people has been crushed, in little more than a decade, and with barely a whimper of opposition, to the point where the sport has almost become meaningless. What once was a sport accessible for all is now a hobby for those who can afford it, and that is both scandalous and tragic.

What is the meaning of football now? Simple, to make vast profits. This is not a revelation. The people who run the game let us know this. Every fan who attends matches will also tell you that football's a business. That's why they pay a fortune for tickets. That's why they buy the team shirt with all the trimmings once or twice every season and subscribe to cable television. The phrase "But football's a business now" is one that gets bandied about on a regular basis in defence (yes defence) of how the modern game is run. And that's it, argument over. Stop complaining and accept reality. Whatever the complaint might be about the integrity of the game, the phrase "But football's a business now" will soon finish all debate. It's an argument that tells fans to forget about the heart and soul of the club they support, and to accept the purpose and reality of the modern game. The purpose of the modern game being solely to exploit the gullible consumer, and the reality being that enough fans are docile enough to simply accept it. And consumers don't get more gullible than us football fans. You only have to look at the food that supporters eat at half-time to realise that they will put up with anything, and then go back for more. Recently, it seems that fans have started to make a bit more noise about the high cost of following their team. However this little bit of noise doesn't worry the clubs too much, as they know that their addicts will still come back for more.

So the question to my fellow supporters is simple: Why do you keep going back for more? If football is just a business, and you know that it's just a business, why go along with it? Why don't you turn the tables back on them? The business world is fickle and unmerciful, and as fans we're the financial backers who the football industry depends on. They are totally at our mercy. So if your football club is making unrealistic financial demands on you, then ask yourself whether or not this business is becoming too expensive for you to carry on financially backing it? Maybe we should all be businessmen and think of ourselves? It's the way I feel about the game these days, so I'm going down the business route, along with everyone else within football.

I'm going to think about my bank balance only. Therefore, being a shrewd businessman I believe it makes sense to abandon this over-expensive product and withdraw my custom. I'm not anti-business because we all have to make a living and prosper. It's just that when I was a kid I didn't feel inspired to put up posters of Donald Trump on my wall, or pay good money to watch Ted Turner hold a board meeting in front of an adoring crowd.

Anyone reading this book who feels indifferent to the corporate takeover of a sport that was once known as 'the People's Game' might point out that there are more important issues in the world than those of us who can't afford to watch football anymore. Well, anyone who would think along those lines would be right. I would tend to agree, that starving children in Africa is more scandalous and shameful than the price of a football ticket. But we'll leave that subject for people like Sir Bob Geldof to inform us on. So for this book we'll stick to football. Secondly, what the bloody hell are you doing reading a book about football when you'd rather be reading one about saving the whale and the hole in the ozone layer?! Go and get a refund now before you damage the book and they refuse to give you back your money. For those of you who lost the receipt, or spilt herbal tea on the front cover, I'm afraid that there is no chapter highlighting the threat of extinction to the orang-utan. But read on anyway. Because the football world mirrors wider society – a lot of the time in a negative way, but also in a positive way.

If British football is overrun with advertising and greed then maybe it's because Britain has become a more commercial, superficial place to live in. But if racism at football is no longer acceptable at our stadiums then maybe it's because British society has become less tolerant of such bigotry. The main principle in football right now is no different to big businesses all over the world, and is also a principle that governments stand by. That principle being: anything that brings in money is beneficial no matter what the consequences. The export of arms from the UK is seen as good for the economy while ignoring the damage this trade brings to the world and the number of lives it destroys. Then of course we send soldiers out to die, when the people we sold the weapons to in order to murder people suddenly turn out to be murderous tyrants. The short-term economy is also put ahead of the welfare of the planet's environment. I know that's an extreme comparison to make in relation to football. No football club is responsible for the slaughter of innocent civilians or for destroying a rain forest. But it's the same line of thinking, in that money comes ahead of every other principle. Advertising is seen as good for football. Sometimes it is, and their money can go to fund good causes within a community. Lower division clubs rely on advertising for their very survival. But what if advertising goes so far as to reduce the capacity of a stadium in favour of advertising hoardings that keep out thousands of fans? This actually happens in the European Champions League. Can replacing fans for the benefit of commercial hoardings really be good for a spectator sport? The genius behind it all is that now many fans view football with the same one-dimensional attitude: anything that brings money in is good for the club. Even if the thing that brings money into the club further takes away the very soul and aesthetics of the game, and further alienates the supporter. Some football fans now talk like bank managers or club directors in regards to what's best for their club, and that really is frightening.

Among the new breed of consumer, there are bound to be many fans on the opposite side of the fence to me. Well I hope that by reading this book they will understand some of the issues as to why many fans are turning their backs on the game. Sorry, let me rephrase that – trying to turn their back on the game. In a recent football-related conversation, I told a friend that "I've had it with football." My friend replied with "You've not had it with football. You're just a football cynic." The bad news is that my friend was 100% right. Once football is in your blood it's virtually impossible to abandon it outright. No one who has ever been obsessed with football can completely stop caring. If someone could forget the game and not even look back, I would question their passion in the first place.

I try to do my bit by not attending many games or purchasing club merchandise. As I've already said, common sense tells me that I should now abandon the industry completely. That's the way it should be with a business if they treat their customers in the wrong way. However this problem I'm faced with isn't quite the same thing as being dissatisfied with one supermarket and changing to another. I'm stuck with it, and will support Arsenal and England till the day I die. In 2006 I travelled to Madrid to be at the Bernabeu stadium to see Arsenal play the greatest club side of all time, Real Madrid, and I travelled to Madrid at a time when I've been more disillusioned with football than at any other time in my life. A month later I would then travel on a road trip through Europe to Turin to watch Arsenal play Italian giants Juventus. A month after that I would make the short trip to Paris to be present in the city where Arsenal played their first ever Champions League final. A year later, in 2007, and as fed up with football as ever, I travelled to Holland to watch Arsenal play PSV Eindhoven. To be so disillusioned with something, but still prepared to travel to other countries and spend so much money to follow that same thing is confusing to say the least. A funny kind of business we have here!

Chapter 2
The envy of the world?

"Right now the English Premier League is just about the definition of a great thing... Less than twenty years ago, English football was known more for rabid fans and decrepit stadiums than for the sort of classy crowd that now fills the suites at the stadiums of Chelsea and Manchester United."

Time magazine, May 2007

In 1992 the top division of English football changed hands when the Premier League/Premiership was formed and replaced the old Football League, which had been established since 1888. The reason behind the Premier League was to re-brand football, make the game more commercially viable and to create more wealth for the top clubs. It has achieved its aim – the FA Premier League is indeed a money-making machine. By 2007, according to Deloitte, the revenue of the Premier League clubs was an incredible $2.5 billion a year – and that was before the three year $5.5 billion TV deal that came into effect from the 2007/08 season. The $2.5 billion figure is triple the revenue generated ten years before in 1997, and nearly $1 billion a year more than the world's second most prosperous league – the Italian Seria A. So who can argue with a success story like that?

There is no definitive right or wrong answer as to whether football is better or worse now than it was in years gone by. People do have a habit of romanticising the past and harping back to a golden era that never existed. I'm not going to do that. I'm not going to claim that football was perfect in the days gone by, because it wasn't, far from it. I'm not advocating a return to the days when stadiums were crumbling, when fans felt threatened by other fans, when black players had bananas thrown at them and when Terry Hurlock should have had bananas thrown at him but didn't. Football did need investment and a change of culture. That investment has to come from somewhere and, as a paying fan, I would have happily paid a bit more for a ticket if it meant better facilities and better players from overseas. However the change that has occurred and the financial burden placed upon English supporters has gone beyond all justification. A mix between what we have now and what football was like in the days before the Premier League would have been the perfect compromise in modernising football, whilst also maintaining what was already so great about the sport.

For example, an English game where the standard of football is as strong as anywhere in the world, but where people of all incomes can afford to watch their team play live. A game where the players are high earners in society, but not to the obscene level which distances them from the rest of society. A game where some fans can sing their hearts out on an open terrace, while other fans can sit and watch the game in a more family friendly environment. A game which has good relations with outside commercial interests, but not to the point where the corporate boys who work for the advertisers replace the true supporters in the stadiums. It's the good and bad things about modern football that will be featured in *Theatre of Silence*. A mix between the positive and negative things we have in the modern game, both at home and abroad, should be that compromise. If the bad things about the modern game heavily outweigh the good things, then so be it. The argument therefore is that football has to make some reverse changes or risk losing the support of many more fans like myself.

In 2007 *Time* magazine ran a feature on English football in which it proclaimed the Premier League as being 'the envy of other sports leagues'. Being an American magazine, and with an American way of thinking, *Time* hailed the Premier League as a roaring success for no other reason than for being so financially prosperous. In reality though, the Premier League is the envy of other businessmen – but not football fans in other countries. I really don't think that football supporters in other countries should be looking towards us with any sort of envy. I doubt very much that German football fans, who pay as little as €10 euros to watch their top teams play, feel that much envy towards fans of English clubs who now have to pick and choose their games due to the extortionate cost of tickets. I also doubt that football fans in other countries, who are allowed the freedom to support their teams in an exuberant nature, feel that much envy towards 'classy' English crowds who now sit down in quiet for the whole game. There are only four teams in England who expect to finish in the top four Premier League places every single season: Chelsea, Man United, Liverpool and Arsenal. Does that mean that fans of clubs such as Aston Villa, Bolton, Middlesbrough, Portsmouth, Manchester City, Newcastle United and Sunderland should be envied for following annual mediocrity?

Those who believe the Premier League is such a fantastic product are looking at it only on a financial level and not a social one. More importantly the same attitude is shared by those who run football. It is this attitude alone in which they are potentially digging their own grave. If football can lose the support of a lifelong fan like myself, then what about this new 'classy' crowd that has latched on to the game because of fashion? There is something that hasn't happened in Britain during the years of the Premier League, in which football should fear happening again in the future. It's something that has happened many times before and is something that will no doubt happen again one day – especially in a country in which millions of people are living in debt. The thing I'm referring to is a recession. A wider economic recession within the country could seriously harm football in a way that it never has done before. In the past, football has survived these hard times for two very simple reasons:

1. The game was affordable entertainment. Therefore people could still attend matches even when undergoing hardship.

2. The players' wages were not high enough to burden the club.

Now the opposite is true for both player wages and admission prices. A wider economic recession is a reality that is unavoidable. We don't know when it will happen, or how bad it will be, but history proves that at some point in the future, our country will face some very hard times. The last time we fell on these times was in the early 1990s, around the same time that the Premier

34

League was being formed. During a recession, people will not spend such crazy money to watch football when they are struggling to pay off the bills, the mortgage or the rent. So the consequence for football could very well be half-empty stadiums and players on wage bills higher than the club's weekly revenues. Who will envy the Premier League then? This is why the people who run the game have to abandon the policy of short-term greed, otherwise the bubble could soon explode right in their faces.

Chapter 3
Customer satisfaction...

Many people believe that football clubs are run like banks these days. They certainly never stop thinking of new ways to rip off their customers. As a club member at Arsenal I was forever being sent applications for Arsenal credit cards and Arsenal mobile phones (they still send me junk-mail even though I am no-longer a member).[1] Now they're even asking their fans to go in to the Spanish housing market through a new property scheme: buy a villa in Spain and get a season ticket for free, etc. Well if the clubs are like banks and businesses then I've got an idea. Maybe it's time for them to start sending out customer satisfaction surveys to their club members and season ticket holders. Feel free to fill this in with regard to the club you support:

HOW SATISFIED ARE YOU WITH THE WAY YOUR FOOTBALL CLUB IS RUN?

1. You're satisfied that your football club understands your financial needs?
Very satisfied   Satisfied   Dissatisfied   Very pissed off

---

[1] A friend of mine who supports Middlesbrough was sent an application for a Middlesbrough credit card, which had the marketing slogan *'Every true Boro fan should have one'*. My friend wrote a letter back to the club, informing them that being a 'true Boro fan' has nothing to do with making the club more profitable through credit card debts. Those who did take up the offer, signed up to 19.9% APR – bargain!

2. You're satisfied with your club's dealings in the transfer market?

Very satisfied   Satisfied   Dissatisfied   Very pissed off

3. You're satisfied that your club treats you as a loyal customer?

Very satisfied   Satisfied   Dissatisfied   Very pissed off

4. You're satisfied with your club's appointments in management and coaching staff?

Very satisfied   Satisfied   Dissatisfied   Very pissed off

5. You're satisfied with the players' performances on the pitch?

Very satisfied   Satisfied   Dissatisfied   Very pissed off

6. You're satisfied with your board members, shareholders and directors?

Very satisfied   Satisfied   Dissatisfied   Very pissed off

7. You're satisfied that the people who run your club have respect for the traditions and history of the club ahead of commercialism and corporate priorities?

Very satisfied   Satisfied   Dissatisfied   Very pissed off

HOW STRONGLY DO YOU AGREE OR DISSAGREE WITH THE FOLLOWING STATEMENTS?

1. Most television football pundits could be replaced by a more straight talking and charismatic plank of wood.
Strongly agree   Agree   Disagree   Strongly disagree

2. Robbie Savage belongs in a Zoo.
Strongly agree   Agree   Disagree   Strongly disagree

3. Clive Tyldesley is fair and neutral when he commentates on Manchester United.
Strongly agree   Agree   Disagree   Strongly disagree

4. Ashley Cole is respected more for his integrity as a person than he is for his talent as a footballer.
Strongly agree   Agree   Disagree   Strongly disagree

5. Chelsea have achieved success through shrewd transfer dealings on a tight budget.
Strongly agree   Agree   Disagree   Strongly disagree

6. Food served at football grounds is of a high standard and great value for money.
Strongly agree   Agree   Disagree   Strongly disagree

7. Foreign players at Portsmouth of whom Harry Redknapp once complained, "Don't speak good English", speak better English than Jamie Carragher.
Strongly agree   Agree   Disagree   Strongly disagree

8. Football phone-in presenter Mike Parry is a beacon of football knowledge, a tactical expert, and a fountain of common sense.
Strongly agree   Agree   Disagree   Strongly disagree

9. FIFA President Sepp Blatter sounds less like a man who should be charge of the biggest sport on the planet and more like an internal organ of the body.
Strongly agree   Agree   Disagree   Strongly disagree

An even better idea would be a little bit more democracy. Could we as fans have the opportunity to vote out club directors like building societies do? No doubt there are certain directors out there who wouldn't even get past the first ballot. Sounds like a crazy idea but it's a policy that two of the biggest clubs on the planet employ. At Barcelona and Real Madrid, the supporters are the ones that get to decide who heads the club by voting in a president via a fans' ballot. It could be pointed out that Catalonia is regarded as left-wing, and Barcelona FC simply incorporates the same social ideals as the region. England is a more capitalist society that doesn't quite share the same social principles. To change football in this way would mean changing the whole political ethos of the country right?

Well, no. Germany is considered a capitalist society, and yet Bundesliga rules state that every club must be 51% owned by members and supporters. This is not radical fan power; it's just common sense, as the people who run football clubs should be at the mercy of the true supporters. There's a strong argument that football clubs should be owned by a community, not just a few individuals who have the power to make decisions that effect thousands of people without being accountable. If those elected do a good job the fans will love them and vote them back in. If they don't do a good job and treat the club and the supporters with disrespect, then the fans will have a lot more power than to simply stage the odd protest or sing 'Sack the board' from the stands. Governments rise and fall from this principle and the same thing should happen to the people in charge of running football clubs. Had the fans of the former Wimbledon FC had this power then the directors would not have been able to get away with relocating their club to Milton Keynes and creating a new football club. The same thing would have also applied to the fans of Brighton & Hove Albion, whose owner Bill Archer sold the ground off to developers for personal profit in 1996. Brighton received virtually no money from this sale and have been without a stadium ever since. A similar fate nearly happened to Wrexham FC in 2004, when owner Alex Hamilton tried to evict the club in order to sell the ground off to a property developer – a company owned by a certain Alex Hamilton! In 2005 the High Court ruled that Hamilton's company had improperly acquired the freehold to the ground and Wrexham ended up in the control of administrators. It's quite worrying to think that one person's greed can be so damaging to a community, and this is why fans need more genuine influence within their clubs. An organisation who promote fan ownership of clubs are Supporters Direct and they can be found online at www.supporters-direct.org/

Chapter 4
The only league that counts...

"If tomorrow, business becomes more important than the game itself, then football will no longer exist."

Aime Jacquet – 1998 French World Cup winning manager.

Today it is accepted that the most important thing in football is generating more money than your competition. Therefore I'm not quite sure what Chelsea FC were doing parading the streets of West London on an open top bus after the 2005-06 season. Okay so they may have won some little football championship trophy for only the second time in fifty years, but the fact of the matter is that they should have been crying into their wine glasses. They may have finished first place in the English Premiership in that year, but only finished fifth place in the league that takes first priority. The only league that counts in modern football is the Deloitte football money league. The league that lists the twenty wealthiest football clubs in the world. Step forward the true champions for that year, Real Madrid.

THE DELOITTE FOOTBALL MONEY LEAGUE – FIGURES RELEASED 2006

This table is for annual revenue generated by the club only, not the wealth of whoever owns the clubs. The figure is taken before club expenditure:

1.	Real Madrid	£186.2 million
2.	Manchester United	£166.4
3.	AC Milan	£158.0
4.	Juventus	£154.9
5.	Chelsea	£149.1
6.	Barcelona	£140.4
7.	Bayern Munich	£128.0
8.	Liverpool	£122.4
9.	Inter Milan	£119.7
10.	Arsenal	£115.7
11.	AS Roma	£89.0
12.	Newcastle	£87.1
13.	Spurs	£70.6
14.	Schalke 04	£65.8
15.	Olympic Lyon	£62.7
16.	Celtic	£62.6
17.	Manchester City	£60.9

18. Everton	£60.0
19. Valencia	£57.2
20. SS Lazio	£56.1

Yet when this league was published in 2006 the Real Madrid fans were not out on the streets celebrating their success. They didn't even bother with an open top bus parade and it's sunny in Spain. Hey amigos, you were champions, what was with the long faces? You shouldn't have let the fact that Barcelona kicked your backsides on the football field during this time spoil the party. They could only finish in sixth place in the Deloitte championship, and big deal that they won the European Champions League in the same year as these financial results were published.

The point is how many David Beckham shirts did they sell in that time? Exactly – they're amateurs. Yet despite all this glory the ungrateful Real Madrid supporters were still not happy. Strangely these Madrid fans do not judge success by how much commercial profit the club makes. They only judge success by winning the Spanish league and Champions League.

Don't these people understand the point of football these days? They're as bad as these whingeing Newcastle United fans who are never happy about the state their team always seems to be in. Newcastle made it to twelfth place in the 2006 Deloitte money league, which was a fine effort. Yet their spoilt fans still complain about the fact that they haven't won a domestic trophy of any kind since Elvis was looking for his first major record deal, and by late 2006 the club reported losses of £12 million due to, among other things, a fall in ticket sales. Poor little Porto may have won the Champions League in 2004, but I'm sure their fans would trade in that trophy any day just to be as lucky as supporters of richer Everton, who in 2006 could celebrate their club being a new entry to the Deloitte league at number seventeen. The following year, West Ham United had become a new entry to the Deloitte money league at number nineteen. Not bad for a club who, in the same week these results were published, were stranded in the relegation zone and looking to be on the way out of the Premiership. The reality is that a club like West Ham United are in the Deloitte money league not because of success on the football field, but because they charge their fans an average of over £40 a game, which is unthinkable for all of the other non-English clubs listed in the financial top twenty.

The Deloitte money league has almost taken the tone of being as important, if not more so, than the actual football leagues. It's certainly reported on by the media like a sporting league with news talk such as "Liverpool move up to eighth place... while Arsenal's season gets worse... they've slipped down to tenth." The Deloitte money league has in recent years been the benchmark as to who are considered the biggest clubs in the world. As Manchester United have consistently topped this league in recent years, they have always claimed the title of the world's biggest club. In 2006 Real Madrid could officially claim this title and they finally took the place of Manchester United as the highest revenue club in the world. A year later in 2007, Madrid had stayed on top of the Deloitte money league proving the previous year was not a one-off.

But the point is that Real Madrid have always been the biggest club in the world. Not because they've managed to sell more merchandise worldwide than Manchester United over a two year period, but because they play in an 80,000 Mecca of a stadium and have won a record nine Champions League trophies. I've seen my team play live (and win 1-0) at Madrid's Bernabeu stadium and it's a novel experience. The club has an aura about it that is more intimidating than any other I've been to. I bought my ticket on the black market and had to sit with the home supporters.

Many of them were very smartly dressed and you even see women in mink coats who look like they got lost on the way to the opera and ended up in a football stadium. The level of expectation there is intense. With the exception of a couple of thousand far right-wing ultras the rest of the crowd make very little noise and don't get behind their team. But unlike quiet English grounds it somehow feels intimidating because the Madrid fans sit back in their seats and expect success, and when they don't get it you can feel the tension and anger rise. When Arsenal beat them 1-0 I didn't see too many people around me consoled by the fact that they were the richest club on the planet.

The Champions League is the most prestigious trophy in club football. For the supposed biggest club in the world, Manchester United have won this trophy on two occasions which is less, or no more than the following clubs:

Real Madrid	9
AC Milan	7
Liverpool	5
Ajax	4
Bayern Munich	4
Juventus	2
Inter Milan	2
Nottingham Forest	2
Barcelona	2
Benfica	2
FC Porto	2

I'll admit that Manchester United are a far bigger club than most of the teams on this list and are truly a world super club. Otherwise it would be the same as claiming that Nottingham Forest are as big a club as Barcelona, who at the time of writing have both won the competition twice. But the point is that the benchmark for success should not be based on the marketing ability to sell lots of LA Galaxy/David Beckham shirts to fifteen-year-old girls in Tokyo. There is a thing called the big club factor, and being a big club should be judged on things like history, fan base, tradition, stadium and on-pitch success. Not just marketing and commercialism, because real on-pitch glory outweighs profit. The club I support look certain to top the Deloitte money league in 2008, having recently announced annual revenue of over £200 million. I've heard fellow fans gloat with pride "We're now the richest club in the world." Well hurrah to that. Let's bring out the champagne, and hire the open top bus. Sorry to be a spoiler, but financial success of this kind does not fill me with pride, especially as it's built on corporate priorities and regular match tickets that range from £46 to £94. It fills me with no more emotion than knowing that the computer I own helps make Microsoft prosper. Achievement in the Deloitte money league might be considered by some as the highest honour in the game, but for true supporters, success in football will always be judged the old-fashioned way.

Chapter 5
The Game in the Balance – part 1

In football right now too many things seem so misplaced and out of character with the aesthetics of the sport. From the music the club DJ blares out when a goal is scored, to the manic depressive fans who put everyone on a downer on radio phone-in shows. The positive things about football seem to be so heavily outweighed. So I put this theory to the test. In my left hand I placed what I, as an ordinary fan, consider to be the positives of the modern game mainly since the formation of the Premiership. In my right hand I placed the negatives. Let's have a look at the result:

Positives

Big screen football and illegal foreign channels
International superstars and skill factor
Wembley Stadium
Tackling racism
Lower Division play-offs

Negatives

Player diving & gamesmanship
Television presentation
'Americanisation' of the game
Corporate priorities
24 /7 fixtures
Chelsea FC and billionaire takeovers
Ticket pricing
Cautions and petty laws
The new consumer

Stewarding and security
All-seater stadiums
Overbearing advertising and marketing
Annual kit changes
Shirt numbering
Wage demands
Stadium design and identity
Lack of home-grown players
Radio phone-in shows
Lack of free speech
Player agents
Media scrutiny
Interpretation and rankings
Prawn sandwiches

After this little experiment I was taken to hospital with a suspected torn muscle in my right arm. Luckily I made a full recovery and got back into good enough shape to be able to type up a few details about these positives and negatives. Let's be positive first...

POSITIVES

Big screen football and illegal foreign channels

In the last few years I've gone from being a fan who regularly attended live matches to what they call an 'armchair supporter' (or perhaps now, a 'bar-stool supporter'). In other words – someone who follows their team via a television screen.
When you stop attending live games you become a lot more disconnected with the team you support. I'm not quite as joyous

when they win, and not quite as downhearted when they lose. You also start to come out with these weird phrases, things you never used to say, stuff like "Who are we playing next weekend?"

With the cost of football now so high, many of football's forgotten fans fill up the pubs and bars instead of the rows of plastic seats. Sometimes the atmosphere in certain venues can be more electric than what you might experience in the actual stadiums. I've been in pubs that have erupted in celebration and seen a release of tension and energy that was once familiar during the 'dark days' of football. I encounter a lot of people who actually prefer to follow their team in a pub or bar, because it's far more social and hassle free than going to the game. In a way, terrace culture has survived in these venues for the following reasons...

1. You can stand up if you want to.
2. You can watch the game in the company of your friends.
3. You can decide on the day of the game if you want to go and watch it.
4. It won't cost £40 to get in to the pub.
5. There are no men in orange bibs, telling you what you can and can't say.

So what does it say about the modern game when so many supporters actually prefer watching the game in a pub for these reasons? In this day and age, fans of Premiership clubs are lucky, in that we have the option to follow our teams from the television for virtually every game. This is because many bars and pubs now show Premiership matches on foreign channels, whereas there is a law in the UK stipulating that no British channel can broadcast a live match between 3.00pm and 5.00pm on a Saturday (a law in place to safeguard attendances in other games). The big screens we now have are a new and improved way to watch sport. During a World Cup or European Championship, giant screens are put up all over the country (except in our capital city) and even some cinemas have gone back to the old tradition of showing big games on the silver screen. Sport just like the movies, looks so much better when bigger. However, I shall end this with a strong word of warning: I've been in pubs that have had *'Celebrity Big Brother'* showing on a big screen.

International superstars & skill factor

Those of us, who have issues with the financial and social side of the English game, have to also acknowledge that the standard of domestic football has got better since the formation of the Premier League. This is mainly down to the increase in top quality foreign players. Unfortunately this hasn't made the English league more competitive as a contest, as only a few of the same clubs ever stand a chance of winning the title, but the skill factor and speed of the game has definitely improved. Without the increase in top foreign players, Premiership clubs would stand less of a chance of winning the Champions League, and the worlds' best players should, in theory, benefit England internationals who play their club football with these foreign talents. The England national team has painfully underachieved throughout the Premier League years, but that is probably more down to the dominance of average foreign players who stifle home-grown talent. We love to see Eric Cantona, Gianfranco Zola and Thierry Henry, but not the costly failures such as Bosko Balaban, Winston Bogarde, and Steve Marlet.

English club football suffered and fell behind as a result of the ban on our clubs in Europe between 1985 and 1990. Although English clubs with home grown players have won the Champions League many times in the past, the influence of foreign players since the ban, has been needed to get our teams back to a competitive standard.

impressive (especially when lit a night) and became a British landmark long before the stadium was even near to being finished. The inside of the ground is also excellent and a perfect venue to watch a game of football. We have a great national stadium and that is at least a start. However the next step has to be to develop Wembley as a people's stadium, accessible to everyone. The question is though – how long will that take to build?

Tackling racism

"It [football] is colour blind. When for instance, in the 1970s, the Brazilian military government attempt to 'whiten' the national team, there was a huge popular and successful demand for the return of the black players who had been and were soon again selected on merit."

Melvyn Bragg

One of the worst things about 1970s and 1980s football was the sound of monkey noises from sections of the crowd directed towards black players.

The abuse that players such as John Barnes, Cyril Regis and Luther Blissett had to put up with is now thankfully in the past in English football, a more positive example of how football's had to change with society. Personally I've never heard monkey chanting at any football match in this country and I've been attending games regularly since the year 1986. The only time I've heard this type of racism was when I went to watch AC Milan play Lazio in Italy. Milan player Clarence Seedorf received the ball near the Lazio fans and a loud monkey chant went up by a sizable minority. I and the people I was with looked surprised by this, but to the rest of the crowd this seemed like just a normal part of the Italian game and was not even an issue. In England now that would not be allowed to happen and action would have been taken against

It's somewhat surprising that it has taken so long for the English league to accept foreign players as a normal part of the game. The leagues in Spain and Italy had no issues with fielding the top foreign players from the very formations of their leagues in the 1930s. During the same period in time it would have been inconceivable that English teams would have regularly recruited players from overseas, and it highlights arrogance in the English mentality over the years. In the early days of football we considered ourselves to be untouchable. So much so that we didn't even bother to enter the World Cup until 1950. A lot of the time that attitude was justified and even the rest of the world still viewed England as the masters of the game. In 1948 Italy were rated by many as the best team in the world and were also officially the world champions.

In that year, Italy played England who were seen by many as the unofficial world champions. This high profile game was played in Rome and England humiliated the world champions 4-0. This confirmed to the English the belief that they were still the masters of the game they invented. It wasn't until the famous England v Hungary game at Wembley in 1953 that this belief was finally blown to pieces in dramatic fashion. At the time, the Hungarians were the superpowers of European football and boasted one of the world's greatest ever players in Frederick Puskus. England were destroyed 6-3 by Hungary in what was the first time the inventors of the game had ever been beaten on home soil. Eighty-one years of home superiority crushed in a game that cruelly proved to the English that the foreign players had developed better technique and were the new masters of the game. Without this attitude of superiority, foreign players would have been a regular part of the English game decades before, but it wasn't until the late seventies when it became normal to see players from overseas play for English teams.

At Highbury I saw Dennis Bergkamp make his debut for Arsenal back on the first day of the 1995-96 season against Middlesbrough. He failed to score and the press mauled him for supposedly making an unimpressive performance. My eye-witness impression was that of a player with more skill and finesse than I'd ever seen before on a football pitch. Watching him play live for the first time was an education in touch, passing ability and all-round technique. The likes of Bergkamp have also set a better example to home-grown players through their professionalism of the game and dedication to their own career. Whereas the English players had a reputation for boozing and eating the wrong foods, the foreign players appeared to take their profession more seriously and looked after their bodies. As a result of this the English players have had to improve their habits and diets. Tony Adams and Lee Dixon have both claimed that Arsene Wenger's ideas on nutrition and fitness added another two years to their professional careers. Dennis Wise once commented that when Gianfranco Zola first came to Chelsea in the late 1990s he put the other players to shame with his professionalism.

Some overseas players in England also speak better English than their home-grown counterparts. After playing in the English league for many seasons Liverpool's German midfielder Dietmar Hamann complained "I still can't understand Jamie Carragher!" In fact this was a widespread opinion from most of Liverpool's foreign players who had mastered the English language but hadn't quite mastered extreme scouse. If it makes them feel better, I can't understand Jamie Carragher either.

Wembley Stadium

This is a very hard one to put down on a list of positives and could just as easily be listed as a negative. First of all, things went from bad to worse in regards to completing the stadium on time and on budget. Inevitable comparisons were made with the Millennium Dome in terms of cost and failure to meet deadline. Most people are now of the opinion that because Wembley wasn't built on time we will also bugger up the Olympics in 2012. The only defence then that can be made for the construction of the Wembley Stadium project is that when landmark structures get built, history shows that the development doesn't always go smoothly or to schedule.

Since the opening of the stadium, the cost and distribution of tickets has been a disgrace and represents so much that is wrong with the modern game. Empty seats have been a regular sight at many games that have been officially sold out. This is because genuine supporters don't get allocated enough tickets while the Club Wembley Members (an exclusive club for people who pay £10,000 for the right to buy a ticket) don't always bother to buy the tickets that are offered to them. These tickets are allocated only to the members and cannot be sold to anyone else even if it means empty spaces in the stadium. Corporate 'supporters' are given priority over the real fans of the two competing teams, which is scandalous given that Wembley was built partly with charity money from organisations such as the National Lottery.

For the 2007 FA Cup Final at Wembley, ticket prices were 40% higher than for the 2006 FA Cup Final which was played in Cardiff. A very limited number of 'cheap' seats were sold at £35 while the next prices up were at £60, £80 and £90. FA chief executive Brian Barwick claimed that the prices were "*sensible, affordable, and very competitive*", although Chairman of the Football Supporters Federation Malcolm Clarke responded to this by saying "*When they say that tickets are competitively priced they are comparing the prices with the Premier League. It does not matter if you have a nice stadium and a big game, if you do not have the money, that's it.*" Another spokesman for the FA defended the 2007 Cup Final ticket prices on BBC Radio 4, by claiming that a limited number of tickets actually went on sale for as little as £17. What he forgot to mention was that these £17 tickets were the cheapest prices for juveniles!

So what is so positive about the new Wembley Stadium? Well, despite all the flaws and difficulties it is still a fantastic stadium – arguably the best in the world. The giant arch looks

Lazio. Many of Europe's leagues have this problem, with the Spanish La Liga being the most high profile.

In 2006 when playing for Barcelona, Cameroon striker Samuel Eto'o threatened to walk off the pitch after loud monkey chants were directed at him by large sections of Real Zaragoza supporters. Real Zaragoza's punishment for this was a 6,000 euro fine, an amount less than some of their top players would get paid in a week. This was not an isolated incident for Samuel Eto'o who had also received racist abuse at other Spanish football grounds from fans of Real Madrid, Athletico Madrid, and Racing Santander to name a few. England still has plenty of racists at football grounds but the authorities have been coherent and clear about the consequences if this racism is displayed in any way. The *Let's Kick Racism Out of Football Campaign,* which was founded in 1993, has been the most prominent voice and is an organisation funded by the main governing bodies of English football including the Premier League, FA and PFA.

People on the outside say that racism is still rife within football. Whether that be true or not, those who say such things should take a look at the industries they work in and see how integrated they are. Football is one of the few things we have where people of all races actually mix together. A game of park football in London will be far more racially integrated than for example a party held for workers of any media or advertising company. How many black people do you see walking around in suits in the city square mile of London? How many black people do you see in the Houses of Parliament? Look around your office and count how many black people there are working with you (don't count the black receptionist who's there to make the company look like an equal opportunity employer). I've done work for the film and television industry since the year 2000. I've worked on hundreds of different TV and film productions and in that time I've not seen one black director or one black producer.

People complain that there's too much football on TV. Whether that's the case or not, at least it's a time where you actually see black people on the television in a starring role, other than MTV and *Crimewatch*. Rather than being a 'who you know' industry, in football ability and character are all that matters.

Yes there is a lack of black people in the very top jobs in football. The Premiership has virtually no history of black managers other than Dutchman Ruud Gullet and Frenchman Jean Tigana. I've never seen or heard of any black board member, director or executive of a football club. But this is the business side of the game, and it's no surprise that the people who run football clubs tend to look the same as the people who run other big corporations.

So there is still a way to go in football in terms of equality. No British Asian has yet made the highest level or become a household name. For the amount of British Asians who play the game it's surprising to say the least. But I know one of the problems as to why this is. A few years ago I used to play for a predominantly Asian Sunday league team called Finsbury Park Monarchs. We played in a North East London league at Hackney Marshes. The teams we played against in this league were all integrated with white and black players. The Asian players, mostly Indian and Bangladeshi, were a bit smaller and less physical but they made up for it with skill and we would finish in mid-table and make the odd cup final. I never saw one example of racism directed towards our team (apart from the time when one of our Indian defenders called one of our white midfielders a 'paki'). However the Finsbury Park Monarchs decided to switch leagues and go and play in the Asian league in North West London.

All of a sudden the non-Asian players in the team like myself were then classed as 'foreigners' and we were only limited to four 'foreigners' to a game. Not for the first time in my life either, having already been classed as a 'foreigner' in the London Greek

League. Maybe I should set up a London Aryan League and see how that goes down? *Sorry mate, only four players allowed who don't have blonde hair and blue eyes!* The reason this is a problem for the development of Asian players is that it's isolationist. Scouts searching for talent are less likely to watch games in these types of leagues. There's no use in running away from the realities of what you would be up against in professional football. The best in football will include big ugly white and black guys, and Asians should face up to this reality rather than be left on the outside.

There is also a lack of black and Asian supporters attending professional football matches, and for some football clubs to survive they need to find a way to bring more support in from ethic minorities. A city like Birmingham is 30% non-white but this is not represented in the fan base of the local clubs like Aston Villa, Birmingham City, Wolves, Walsall and WBA. Other struggling clubs like Bradford City, Blackburn, Burnley and Oldham also need to get in more fans from the ethnic minorities of their towns, as there is potential for a huge fan base which these clubs currently lack. In London more than most, football grounds are in communities with large ethnic backgrounds. Again this is not represented in the fans who attend football matches. With London Asians it might come down to the fact that virtually every London Asian I know for some reason has chosen to support Liverpool! It might also come down to ticket pricing, as black and Asian people are among the lower earners in society and football is now a rich man's sport. Arsenal and Spurs pride themselves in having lots of black people who attend games. With these two clubs there is very little recent history of racism, although very small sections of the Arsenal support have been known for anti-Jewish songs that include references to gas chambers. This is no doubt influenced by Spurs fans calling themselves the 'Yids', but singing about Hitler and gas chambers is prejudice that goes way beyond football rivalry (this is not to be confused with a lot of Arsenal chants that include words like 'yids' and 'yido' when Arsenal fans sing these songs they are referring to Spurs, not Jews).

But even though Arsenal and Spurs have many black fans who attend games the number is still hugely under-representative of the area as well as of the colour of the players who represent the teams. At Arsenal and Spurs the integration comes in the pubs and bars of the surrounding areas. In these venues, a more equal mix of white and black people watch the matches together on the big screens. That is real integration and comes about simply through football. So although the game still has problems with racism the positives outweigh the negatives. Football has done so much for integration and deserves more credit for this than to simply be labelled as racist. In the football grounds themselves the authorities have made a real effort to combat racism and they have been effective.

Lower division play-offs

Technically the play-offs shouldn't be included in the list as it's based on the positives and negatives beyond 1992 and the formation of the Premier League. The lower division play-offs were first played in 1986. But it's included because they have grown in this time and have become an accepted part of the English football calendar. So high are the stakes of being in the Premiership, the lower division play-offs have become even more intense and desperate, resulting in some great matches. The play-off final to gain promotion to the Premiership is now the most financially rewarding single match of any sport in the world and reported to be worth around £45 million. But the real reward for the fans is the knowledge that a win in this one game will mean that their team will be playing league football against the likes of Manchester United, Liverpool, Arsenal, Everton, and Spurs.

Football at its best is about excitement and drama. Excitement and drama come about through a level of competition that is passionate, equally matched and competitive. The play-off finals are the promotion decider for the three lower divisions in England. The top two teams in the league automatically go up to the division above leaving the next four teams to battle it out for the last promotion place. One very predictable argument that occurs every year during the play-offs will be when the manager of the team that finishes third complains that they should be automatically promoted, and shouldn't have to play a competition involving the teams that finished below them.

It's a pointless argument as the rules of the league are set out clearly at the start of each season. The four teams that finish below the top two have to compete in a play-off: end of argument. We all know that the same managers who complain that the play-offs are unfair would not voice the same opinion if they were in charge of teams that finish in the positions below third place. It's very common for the teams that finish third in the table to lose in the play-offs, while the team that finishes sixth can very often win promotion. This is usually put down to psychological reasons as the third placed team has the disappointment on missing out on second place, while the team that finishes sixth can feel less pressure to succeed, and so are able to play with greater freedom. The teams that finish sixth and who end up winning, often prove as worthy of being in the Premiership as the teams who finish in the top two. In 2005 West Ham United won promotion via the play-offs, while Sunderland gained automatic promotion. The next season in 2005-06, West Ham finished ninth place in the Premiership while Sunderland finished bottom with a miserable fifteen points, earning an unwanted record for the least amount of points in a Premiership season.

The reason for the play-offs is very simple. They are there to keep the interest in lower division football intense throughout the whole season. It plays the most important part in preventing the small clubs from going out of business altogether. In the lower divisions the season is never over for any club and there is always something to fight for if a team can find a good spell of form. A team can rise from a relegation position to a play-off place in a very short period of time. In 2004 Crystal Palace went from being near the relegation zone in Division 1 (now the Championship) to being in the Premiership in the space of about three months. What a contrast to the predictable nature of the Premiership and other top leagues in Europe.

NEGATIVES

Player diving and gamesmanship

"Players are conning each other, I'm glad I'm not playing anymore, especially in the Premiership. I can't get my head round a player who rolls around then gets up thirty seconds later. I'd be embarrassed. Lads I've played with go down like they've been shot and it drives me crazy."

Roy Keane

Watching skilled athletes rolling around on the ground pretending to be hurt is one of the most pathetic sights in modern football. It would create value from a comical point of view if the offending players didn't get away with it so often. When watching a game as a neutral you can sit back and laugh when a player embarrasses himself by whipping the head back and doing a swan dive. Most of the time it looks so unconvincing, it's surprising that referees fall for it.

As someone who's played football I know that when you're hurt the last thing you do is roll around on the ground several times and aggravate the injury. I can't name any other sport in which the players fake an injury in order to gain an advantage or to punish an opponent. The 2006 World Cup was regarded by many as the worst example of player diving, but it probably wasn't any more frequent or extreme than any other time in recent football history. The only difference now is that people are getting sick and tired of it, because it's ruining what should be the greatest sport in the world.

The football authorities have been completely inept in dealing with the problem of player gamesmanship of this kind. Since the late 1990s FIFA has run a fair play campaign which has been all gestures and no action. FIFA think that the best way to clamp down on bad sportsmanship is by having kids bring on banners reading FIFA FAIR PLAY before a game. Sorry to be a cynic, this type of gesture doesn't stop bad sportsmanship. Footballers only react to gestures such as fines and suspensions. Most sensible people know that there's an easy way to stop this cheating overnight with a simple law involving video evidence. If a player is found guilty of cheating by diving or feigning injury then he receives something like a three match ban. If a player is found guilty of the same offence twice in a season then he receives something like a five match ban. Brian Clough once commented that if a manager was fined a week's wages for every time one of his players dived then it would solve the problem overnight. Obviously this is too sensible for the likes of FIFA who would rather display meaningless fair play gestures than to bring in laws that would actually make the game fairer. The football authorities are certainly quick to punish players for bad tackles, shows of emotion and even voicing an opinion. Yet when a player tries to get another player punished by feigning injury the authorities do virtually nothing.

An even better law to stop injury feigning and diving would be legalised thuggery! Yes legalised thuggery, now hear me out. If a player pretends that he's hurt his leg and been found guilty of cheating, then the leg should be made to pay the price. Let's say for example that a player has gone down in a crumpled heap without any contact. He holds his shin in pain and slyly looks up to see the opposition player get a caution for an offence he never committed. The diver thinks that he's won the day, however the FA study the videotape and judge that he feigned injury to get a fellow professional penalised. As a punishment, the player who got the caution then gets to kick that player in the shin for real and as hard as he likes! I would recommend that Sky Sports could even show this rough form of justice on pay per view.

Laws aside, the players themselves should have more professional pride than to dive and feign injury. Old pros such as Roy Keane, Terry Butcher, Stuart Pearce, Julian Dicks and Tony Adams never once lowered themselves to that kind of cheating. Players who dive can also get themselves a reputation that works against them when they are genuinely fouled. England striker Andy Johnson is someone who has been such an expert at diving and deceiving the referee, that whenever he does get fouled there are immediately cries of 'cheat'. Robert Pires and David Ginola also had many genuine free-kick and penalty appeals turned down due to reputations for being divers. When playing for Newcastle, Ginola once got sent off for receiving two yellow cards handed out to him for diving, when in fact TV replays showed that he had been genuinely fouled by the defender. He had become the boy who cried wolf and he had nobody to blame but himself. Players go down too easily as contact alone is seen as a good enough reason to fall over, even though football's supposed to be a contact sport. The footballing authorities should take the blame for this as they've gone too far in making football a sport where a player feels justified in falling to the ground after minimal contact has been made.

Diego Maradona was the greatest player in the world during the 1980s and arguably the best player of all time. In the prime of his career one of the most impressive aspects of his game was his ability to stay on his feet and not go down when he was fouled. It was a part of his game that was to his advantage, as some of the best goals or set-ups he ever produced were times when he would keep his balance whilst being fouled. It was an honest schoolboy-like approach to playing football, but during the 1990 World Cup that part of his game changed, and Maradona was a worse player for it. In that tournament Maradona had reduced his style of play to diving whenever he thought he could con the referee. He would no longer try and stay on his feet when challenged, and the end result was that he never made the runs or passes that he was still capable of doing. It was sad to see such a great player still in the prime of his career lose such a noble and effective part of his game in favour of a pathetic style of cheating. The World Cup of 1990 was a time when diving and feigning injury was increasing and becoming a big problem within the sport. Had FIFA heavily clamped down on it at that time then I don't think it would be such a big problem now.

Diving has become such an accepted part of football that conning the referee is now considered a skill. Players are referred to as clever when they gain a penalty through diving, though it shouldn't be considered to be anything other than shameful cheating. If it is so clever why not just go the full way and have a Dive of The Month competition on *Match of The Day* (we could judge the winner by holding up scorecards). In the 2002 World Cup Michael Owen was considered 'clever' for diving and gaining England a penalty kick which ultimately won us the game against Argentina. Yet had it been an Argentina player that dived he would have been described as devious, dishonest and a slimy con artist. People try and justify this kind of cheating by saying that the footballers are under enormous pressure to win games. If that's the case then maybe we should all live our life by the same principle. Modern life is competitive and financially times are hard for many. Therefore due to these pressures it's perfectly acceptable for me to cheat on my tax return this year. As long as I can get away with conning the Inland Revenue then fair enough, right? Somehow I don't think that the judge would accept that line of defence. Trying to get opponents penalised through diving and feigning injury should never be an accepted part of the game. If getting someone punished for something they're innocent of is deemed as acceptable, then what kind of example is football sending out to children and the rest of society?

Television presentation

"I was doing the TV panels with the likes of Jimmy Hill, Jack Charlton, Malcolm Allison and Bill Shankly. It was like the football's *Who's Who* on the box at the time, and I was usually the one who said something that was seized upon by the press. I never did see the point of going on television, expected to voice an honest opinion, and then saying next to nothing or being cautious and particularly careful just to avoid upsetting somebody. There are too many supposed pundits who do exactly that now. What a life! Get yourself on TV, get paid a small fortune, smile a lot and say next to nowt. Now that's nice work if you can get it."

Brian Clough

What Brian Clough was referring to here, is that for some reason, Sky Sports, ITV and the BBC choose presenters and analysts who can make an art form out of sitting on the fence. To put it in very simple terms, the pundits of years gone by were more entertaining and straight talking. Ian St John and Jimmy Greaves were the main faces of football television coverage during the

1980s. The Saint and Greaves were both football legends turned presenters who fans felt an affinity for because they came across as down-to-earth and carried the image of two old men discussing football in a pub or a bookmakers. Jimmy Greaves was not the most presentable man to ever appear on TV, however he was funny, forthright and had charisma. The two men combined brilliantly as the Saint would spend half the show laughing at Greavsie's comments. That was a time before television bosses across the board decided that nobody over the age of fifty was allowed to be seen on any programme other than the Queen's Speech and repeats of *Dad's Army*.

On BBC during the same period, Jimmy Hill and Terry Venables were the main football pundits, with Des Lynam presenting. It's easy to criticise someone like Jimmy Hill, but as a TV personality, he never lacked a different opinion and was never boring. Terry Venables would tear his hair out over Jimmy Hill's comments and the two of them would regularly enter into a heated debate. Their style is certainly in contrast with today's pundits who all nod and agree with each other, and tell us very little that those of us who aren't 'experts' don't already know. It's not to say that every one of them is boring because there are exceptions. For example, Alan Hansen and Ian Wright are both honest and will speak their mind which is what the viewer wants from them. Another worthwhile pundit is Sky Sports Chris Kamara whose enthusiasm and 1980s show-glow hairstyle and moustache make him a likeable character. With too many other pundits however, the TV companies think they have to play it safe and choose people who fit the middle of the road environment that currently dominates football. It appears that the main criterion for being a TV sports analyst is a nice haircut, a nice suit and a lack of any presence or charisma.

The only person that most TV analysts will speak their mind about during a game will be the poor old referee. The experts in the studio will look at about ten clips of an incident in slow motion, then all agree that the referee made a bad decision and is incompetent. With everyone else they will try and be as safe as they can by using clichés that don't quite say it all. Such as:

"He seemed to go down quite easily"
He's a diving cheat.

"They're going through a transitional period right now"
They used to be a good team. Now they've fallen apart.

"He'll be disappointed with that effort"
He gets paid forty grand a week and he can't score from two yards out.

Modern football coverage can, at times, be over the top and very hard on the eyes, ears and brain. This is supposed to be the golden age of television sports coverage. But only in the sense that there are many more live games on TV and the technology is far superior compared to years gone by. The high quality tracking cameras and slow motion replays can give us a better insight into a live game which of course is a good thing. But sometimes the way the technology is applied can also make for uncomfortable viewing and this is mainly through the editing. I've got good eyesight but even my eyes can't cope with the amount of edits per second and the jerky cameras. Unless a person has superhero eyesight that has the power to slow down motion then the majority of after-match football clips are completely unwatchable (these clips are usually in the form of the tedious and overused musical montage). A montage of football clips will have as many edits per second as an MTV video. This can be as much as two edits per second. Two edits per second is no way to watch sport, in fact it's no way to watch anything. I've closed my eyes in cinemas during some films where the editing is so fast that it's impossible to have any idea of what is happening. It's like watching a movie on DVD with the fast forward button on. Technically this style of editing is very impressive, but as a viewer I find it very hard to watch. In old style football presentation we simply got shown the best of the action without any fancy gimmicks.

So if I had my way I would make changes to the way football is presented on television, starting with boring pundits and fancy editors. Another change I would make would be that English commentators have to be shown the door. With Clive Tyldesley I would recommend that door read ROOM 101. And their replacements should be foreigners. Well why not? Its okay for players, managers, and even club owners to come from overseas, so why not the commentators too? They're better at it than our home-grown announcers. They've got more flair and exuberance, and what better way for a commentator to greet a goal than the South American style GOOOOOOOOOOOAAAAAALLLLLL... GGG... GOOOOAAAALLLLL. Sky Sports actually employ this tactic by using fans as commentators, as opposed to the regular commentary. It's a promising idea but it doesn't really work, mainly because those involved in the commentary have absolutely no talent. These biased fans scream when a goal is scored but it's hard on the ears and they sound like a cat being tortured or a Christina Aguilera record (or a cat being forced to listen to a Christina Aguilera record).

The South American style GOOOOAAAAAAALLLLL... has an operatic quality about it but, more than anything, these amigos sound like they're having a great time when calling the action – much more so than some of our English commentators who can sound so dull and uptight. Our home-grown commentators are also so quick to condemn everything from a pitch invasion to a player who shows emotion and exuberance. John Motson made his name in the 1970s when he commentated on a famous FA Cup giant killing, when non-league Hereford beat mighty Newcastle United

2-1 after being a goal down. The goals were greeted by the famous sight of hundreds of parka jacket clad kids running on to the pitch in celebration. It's footage the BBC repeat on a regular basis as iconic images associated with FA Cup giant killing. In this day and age though the Hereford pitch invaders would now be deemed to be committing a serious criminal offence. This offence is punishable with a fine or custodial sentence, plus a place on the hooligan register and ban from every football ground in the country. This strict attitude in football is now reflected in the commentary. If the same attitude were around in 1966 then I would hate to think what Kenneth Wolstenholme's immortal lines in the World Cup Final would have sounded like… *'And some people are on the pitch. They think it's all over…What a disgrace…they should not be on the pitch…where are the stewards…Dear oh dear…They've ruined the game.'*

Kenneth Wolstenholme was a fine example of how British football commentary hasn't always been dull and uninspiring. He, along with Brian Moore and David Coleman were all masters of their profession and their voices had a British movie star quality about them. They also had a comic side and light-heartedness in their tone. In the 1966 FA Cup final Everton beat Sheffield Wednesday 3-2 after coming back from being two goals behind. Everton's equalising goal sparked a one man pitch invasion from a fat, bald, suited-up scouser. He was chased from one half of the pitch to the other by police whom he avoided like a rugby player who brushes off the defence en route to scoring a try. Wolstenholme's commentary for this incident highlights a more relaxed attitude to the time and a sense of fun. He simply commented on the action in front of him. As one policeman rugby tackled the Everton fan on the edge of the 25 yard box, Wolstenholme shouted out *"And a great tackle. Almost on the line."* There's only one commentator around today who has the same style persona and that is Stuart Hall, the old *It's a KNOCKOUT* presenter. He works on the radio for BBC Five Live and has that old-fashioned dramatic voice along with a sense of fun. But they only let him commentate on low profile matches (usually Manchester City games) and it seems like he's just there as a gimmick rather than a serious commentator. Funny thing is though, despite the fact that he's not taken seriously, Stuart Hall is arguably the most entertaining and eloquent commentator they have.

Clive Tyldesley is rated by many as the top TV commentator. Indeed, he has won awards for his work, and he does have a very good knowledge of football tactics. Okay that's the plaudits over with – I and many others find his style of commentating exasperating, especially when along the lines of *"Here we are in this football coliseum, where these two teams of gladiators are set to battle it out to the finish in front of a baying crowd."* Or even… *"Welcome to Old Trafford the Theatre of Dreams, as tonight's stars get ready to act out in front of a packed auditorium. Which one of the performers is going to write the script blah blah blah…"*

This type of metaphoric commentary could possibly work if done by Orson Wells or Laurence Olivier. Those two actors carried a talent that should also be the basic requirement of a football commentator – a great voice. Clive Tyldesley is a self-confessed boyhood fan of Manchester United. This certainly shows when he commentates on Manchester United. Actually, it shows when he commentates on a game which has bugger-all to do with Manchester United. *"The crowd here at Rochdale just 3,000. That's 87,000 less than you can cram in to the Nou camp stadium…Which reminds me…who can ever forget that balmy night in Barcelona when Manchester United scored those two goals in injury time."* Clive Tyldesley has got himself such a reputation for blabbing on about that "balmy night" in the Nou Camp, that he now has to give money to charity for every time he mentions it in his commentary (someone hit the jackpot there). Here is my entry to the 'Clive Tyldesley Book of Easy-To-Make

Up-Metaphors – Volume 3 *"Well Ron, football commentary is an art form but right now we're lacking in Rembrandts and Michelangelo's."* The art of sports commentary is to have a dramatic voice and to project genuine emotion.

Today it is too focused on fancy lines and 'clever' metaphors. Football commentators also like to go over the top in the words they use to describe a good piece of play. These words such as 'sumptuous', 'mouth watering', 'sublime' and 'sizzling' seem more suited to a Sunday roast than football.

British football coverage is growing paranoid about broadcasting anything so slightly controversial. If there is a streaker on the pitch the camera will now focus on another part of the stadium and away from the incident. This rule is meant to keep off air anything that looks as if it condones what is banned in football. So by the same principle Jessica Alba could run on the pitch at Old Trafford wearing just her earrings and yet we'd see nothing. And they class that as entertainment – for our viewing pleasure? So the question is – what's the more criminal? Okay I'll admit that Jessica Alba is unlikely to do this! Most streakers don't look like Hollywood actresses, but there have been some good ones over the years. There can even be value in a naked fat bloke running on to the pitch and being chased by stewards. During a Chelsea v Arsenal match in 2005, a bare-arsed Arsenal fan ran on to the pitch with the message *You can stick your Russian roubles up your...* along with an arrow running down his back and pointing to his posterior! This wasn't shown by Sky Sports who instead focused on the Chelsea team bench which showed Jose Mourinho laughing at the incident. Football is uncensored when the TV coverage comes from Europe or South America. When football is broadcast to us from other countries we get English commentary but the producing is done by a TV company in whatever country the game is played in. During the Euro 2004 final in Lisbon, a Spanish man ran on to the pitch and was chased by the stewards in

Keystone Cop fashion. As the English commentator apologised for the uncensored Portuguese TV coverage, the viewer witnessed the pitch invader run towards one of the goals at high speed and jump into the top corner of the net. Where I watched the game the whole room cheered on this terrific long jump, while the English commentator came out with the usual "No one wants to see this sort of thing at football".

It's also a good bet that when the Spaniard flew into the top corner of the net the South American commentators shouted out GOOOAAAAALLLL. As a TV viewer I would like to be treated like an adult and do not need to be protected from these 'shocking images'.

So there you have it. Football presentation on television could be improved and the BBC, ITV and Sky should make me head of their sports coverage! I'd have operatic Brazilians shouting down your television screens within weeks. GOOOAAAAAALLL.

'Americanisation' of the game

For the most part I'm not anti-American. I've liked most Americans that I've met, and any country that gives the world blue jeans, rock and roll and Hollywood has a lot of good things going for it. As for their sports, they carry a certain image and style which is different to the rest of the world, but it's a style that doesn't really work when copied by Leyton Orient. The best example of what I mean by this is the playing of music whenever a goal is scored, which we now have at many football grounds. The sound of the crowd cheering a goal is now drowned out by loud music that blares over the thousands of voices in the stadium. A football match for the most part is eighty-eight minutes of nothing happening and two minutes of drama. Drama climaxing with perhaps a goal or two being scored, and yet this climax of a game is now being crowned by '*Let me entertain you*' from Robbie Williams. Who was it that came up with that idea? The idea that a second-rate pop song is more fitting to the glory of a goal than the sound of a roaring crowd is perverse. So far the really big Premiership clubs haven't taken to playing music as yet, but many other Premiership clubs do, along with lots of lower division teams. I dislike this trend so much that in the 2004-05 Premiership season I was happy to see Norwich City get relegated, for no other reason than their annoying habit of playing crap music every time they scored a goal at home. So Delia Smith, take note of Morrissey – hang the DJ.

Other such Americanisms include cheerleaders before the game or at half-time. Only the cheerleaders we football fans get are not the Playboy standard vixens who jump up and down for the likes of the Dallas Cowboys. No, we get twelve-year-old girls! This isn't just a Premiership thing and again is probably more common in the lower divisions.

This attempt at razzmatazz is a hopeless cause at the likes of Macclesfield, Grimsby and Hull. These poor girls come on to the pitch at grounds such as Hartlepool and look absolutely freezing. Cheerleaders in Hartlepool should actually be running out in pullovers, leg warmers, and carrying a mug of hot chocolate. It's certainly a long way from the days when brass bands used to perform on the pitch before the game. At least there was meaning to those bands as some of them had historic connections with the clubs. I suppose the basic problem with cheerleading is that it's just not very entertaining. Has anyone ever come home after a football match and commented that "The cheerleaders were on good form today"?

Nothing seems more American than insincere hugging. At a number of clubs, hugging between players goes on just before kick-off as a show of team unity. The beginning of a game can now sometimes look like an emotional episode of Ricki Lake. Cut the hugging out fellas! You don't have to prove to us that you all love one another. Hugging should only be reserved for when you actually do something worthwhile like scoring a goal.

The drummers the clubs employ to irritate everyone can also go as they're not always authentic. I know that if I tried to walk into a football stadium with a drum then I would be turned away at the turnstile. I had a taste of American sport when I was in Texas in 1998. I went to a watch the Texas Rangers take on the Chicago Cubs in baseball. The stadium was fantastic and the game was a great one-off novelty experience.

As for the fans, I got the feeling that many of them were there just for a good excuse to sit down and eat more hot dogs and pizzas. Waiters even come up to your seat to take your order. I don't think I'd like to see that Americanism imported to England though I'm sure one day it will happen. At least it would stop fans leaving the game five minutes before half-time in order to be near the front in the burger queue (it's medically proven that football fans can't go a full ninety minutes without a feed). I suppose I don't like the idea of having waiters come to your seat to take your food order is because it makes the game feel like less of a sport than it already is, and more of a corporate day out.

I wouldn't get rid of every single Americanisation in the game but most don't work in football and should be sent back to Uncle Sam, along with Starbucks, dumbed-down politics, Paris Hilton and Jade Goody (don't let the fact that Jade Goody isn't an American get in the way of a worthy deportation). However the fireworks and the ticker tape can stay, and I can't say enough about the Rocky theme tune that Manchester United have started to play as a build up before each game!

Corporate priorities

A lot of people complain about how football has become too corporate without really understanding just why it's so bad for the game. I'll give you an example of an incident which I think highlights why corporate priorities step on the feet of genuine supporters.

In the summer of 1998 I travelled to France to support England in the World Cup. In England's second group game we were to play Romania in the beautiful city of Toulouse in the south of France. The capacity of the stadium wasn't quite enough to accommodate the thousands of us who had made the journey to Toulouse. I was ticket-less along with quite a few thousand others. The average price for a black market ticket was around 2,000 francs (roughly £200) which was more than we were prepared to pay. An hour before the game and whilst on the look-out for tickets we saw one England fan running away and waving a ticket in the air along with a huge Cheshire grin on his face. It made us laugh when we saw him being hopelessly chased by a fat ticket tout who was waving his hands in the air and shouting "Mon billet... mon billet." Well, I found it funny: at 2,000 francs for a black market ticket who was really the thief? I thought the tout got what he deserved.

Anyway, our search for a ticket was useless. The prices were not coming down and lines of riot police stopped us from getting too near the ground. We sat down by a nearby wall in acceptance that we were going to miss out on a match we had travelled hundreds of miles to see. Our mood wasn't angry or bitter, we were just disappointed. That was until we looked to our left and saw a very large number of coaches that were parked up side by side. These coaches were not England or Romanian supporter's coaches. Each of these coaches had a sign on the front with names like McDonalds, Cannon, Fuji Film, Coca Cola and so on. One large coach then pulled up right in front of us.

Out stepped a group of chino-wearing, shirts-tucked-in, office manager types with Carlsberg baseball caps. They showed their passes at the gate and walked though the line of riot police. None of us spoke a word to one another as there was no need to. It was a classic example of FIFA putting corporate priorities ahead of true football supporters. We felt resentful and had every right to be. We were all part of the official England Members Club (also known as *englandfans*) which is run by the FA. It's the only official way for England fans to purchase tickets for England games. The allocation the FA received was not enough for the amount of members who required tickets, because for the World Cup, FIFA hands out huge allocations of tickets to its corporate sponsors.[2]

Its part of the new football mentality which believes anything that brings money into the game is good for football. Though if money coming into football keeps out true supporters from the game then it can't possibly be considered good for the game. It just generates even more money for those at the top and leaves the real fans on the outside. The 2006 Champions League final was played in an 80,000 capacity stadium in Paris. Yet the fans of the two competing clubs only received 40,000 tickets between them in a game that would easily have sold out three or four times over. So the question is, where did of the other 40,000 tickets go? The same thing happened in the UEFA cup final of the same year when the genuine fans of Middlesbrough and Sevilla only got given a small portion of match tickets. For a fan of Middlesbrough this game would have been the biggest in the club's history. To see their team compete in the UEFA cup final meant everything to these supporters who have followed their team loyally through years of

---

[2] During this piece I originally spelt the word sponsors as 'sponcers'. A terrible example of spelling I admit. But when clicking on spell-check the first word that came up was 'Spongers'. Yep that figures.

mediocrity. During the years of mediocrity these loyal fans are needed. Yet for the good times the same fans are shunned in place of corporate day trippers, so in a sense the real fans can never truly win either way. Even fans of lower league teams now have to put up with the corporate boys stealing all the tickets for the big games. For the first ever Championship Play-off final at the new Wembley Stadium in 2007, just under a third of tickets went to corporate hospitality whilst thousands of loyal Derby County and West Bromwich Albion supporters were left with nothing.

Since France 98 football has become even more directed towards corporate hospitality. During this England v Romania match in Toulouse the amount of tickets that went to hospitality and sponsors was 24%. By the time of the World Cup in Germany 2006, the amount was 31%! That figure is actually more than the amount of tickets given to the fans of the two competing teams which was a mere 8% to each country. This has now gone beyond all reason when the corporate boys get more tickets for major tournaments than the supporters themselves. FIFA president Sepp Blatter insists that "FIFA is proud of these long term partnerships. They are an essential component in staging the World Cup." Interesting, however, the World Cups of years gone by didn't need these essential components in order to stage a football tournament. The perception that there would be no World Cup without this corporate dominance is a lie. The job of the sponsor is to advertise, not take away a large percentage of the tickets from genuine supporters.

A year before the 2006 World Cup the cost of membership to the England Members club went from £25 a term to £60. This fee increase was marketed on the basis that the membership period included the World Cup, and that it was the only official way for fans to obtain tickets for England games. What they didn't yell too loudly was the reality that for each England World Cup game only 8% of tickets at most would be sold to its members. Instead of paying the £60, I decided to withdraw my membership as it was a blatant attempt at cashing in on the World Cup before a ticket had even been put on sale. In hindsight I was right not to rejoin, because when it came down to the sale of World Cup tickets, thousands of loyal England members would be left with nothing. When England members attend games they are credited with loyalty points on their membership. Those with a high number of loyalty points get given a degree of priority when World Cup tickets get put on sale. Away games and friendly matches will normally count for the most loyalty points. However many of those who bothered to support England home and away were considered less loyal than those who work for the sponsors of FIFA. The England Members Club will claim that they are not the ones who make the rules over FIFA's ticketing priority. But they are run by the FA who are a representative of FIFA, and I don't hear too many protests from the English FA about the overbearing corporate side of football. They are all part of the same gravy train. It's because of corporate priorities that I didn't travel to the World Cup in Germany. Before the tournament I was planning a trip with the intention of buying tickets on the black market.

It is common knowledge that the corporate tickets are the ones that get sold on to the touts, which is also something that I've seen with my own eyes during France 98. Real fans don't sell tickets and FIFA rely on the black market in order to fill stadiums as so many corporate freebies end up in illegal hands. I figured that by buying tickets off a tout to go to a FIFA World Cup match, I would be supporting a system that urinates from above on thousands of people like me. Loyal fans get shunned when it comes to the big games in favour of the corporate boys, so then the only logical conclusion is to shun the greedy bastards back. FIFA quite openly has total contempt for ordinary supporters, therefore I had no intention of going along and joining in with their big corporate party.

So back to Toulouse, and one corporate fan showed a lot of class when he walked up to a friend of mine and put a ticket in his hand. My friend asked "How much?" and the man replied "Nothing" and walked off. The rest of us would have to settle for a bar with a television screen. When you travel abroad to watch a football match but miss out on the game itself, it would be nice to think that your place in the stadium is being taken by somebody who really deserves it. On that day in Toulouse and in the current climate in football this is not a realistic consolation.

24/7 fixtures

"In the Mexico 1986 World Cup, TV companies made teams play in Mexico City at midday and with an altitude of 2,500 metres and high levels of smog and humidity. It was inhuman. They sold a bad football product to the world. You have to care for the game and defend it from the outside aggression of commercialisation."

Jorge Valdano – 1986 Argentine World Cup Winner

On October 6th 2007, a record was broken when only one Premiership fixture kicked off at 3.00pm on a Saturday. It was solely down to the influence of television. On that weekend, Sunderland fans were expected to be down in London for a televised game that kicked off at 12.00pm on a Sunday. It only took a month for that record to be equalled, when Derby County v West Ham United was the only 3.00pm fixture on Saturday November 10th. Anyone bother to watch *Match of the Day* that night?

But it's not just the television companies who have this influence on fixtures. The police now dictate the time of fixtures due to the effective and overused 'Health and Safety' excuse. The police insist that high profile fixtures must now be played at 12.45pm so that fans do not have time to drink alcohol before kick-off. Fixtures such as Liverpool v Manchester United, Arsenal v Spurs, Everton v Liverpool, will now always be an early start. However, the police fail to realise that supporters of both sides who want to drink will just stay in the pub for longer after the game and will consume as much if not more alcohol than they would do if the game were a 3.00pm kick off. The fans who watch the games on big screens in nearby pubs will also drink a lot more from an earlier time. Alcohol doesn't create tension or passion in a fixture like Aston Villa v Birmingham City.

As for the hooligan firms who want to fight each other, they will still look for trouble no matter what time the kick-off is. Alcohol plays a smaller role in organised football violence than is the common perception. Hooligans from Liverpool and Manchester or Newcastle and Sunderland will want to fight one another whether they're drunk or sober. A 12.45pm kick-off will finish at roughly 2.45pm. This leaves the rest of the afternoon for the hooligan firms of either side to try and find each other and have a tear-up. In the 2006-07 season, one of the worst incidents of violence, in which ten people received stab wounds, was after a Chelsea v Spurs cup match that kicked off at 12.45pm. Doesn't that one incident alone prove that having early kick-offs in order to prevent disorder is a failed concept?

The best example of this type of overzealous interfering from safety advisors and the police was the local derby between Wrexham and Chester City in December 2005. It was a fixture that hadn't been played for over one hundred years, so naturally there was a lot of excitement between the two sets of supporters. The kick-off time was originally scheduled for the evening of 28th December. It was likely to have been the first sell-out crowd Chester City had had since 2003. Enter the spoilers. The police and the safety advisors recommended that the game should be moved forward to a midday kick-off. Even though the 28th of December was a normal working day so many fans would therefore miss the game. This interfering is so unnecessary because Chester City v Wrexham is not exactly West Ham v Millwall or Boca Juniors v River Plate. By this health and safety principle anything that is remotely high profile must be diluted. For any public event that is popular, the police advice to people is to stay away from the area due to health and safety.

Well, that's everything apart from royal ceremonies. Suddenly then the health and safety obsession goes out the window. For these royal occasions they like the streets to be full to show how much support there is for the monarchy. Did the police or anyone else tell the public to stay away from the Queen's 2002 Golden Jubilee? No, and they wouldn't have dared either. The crowds were massive that day and it was as big a public event as anything that has been held in London. Yet for every other public event from a New Year's Eve firework display to an open air concert, the police will always tell the public to stay away from the area. The health and safety excuse is a very effective way of controlling people and should always be looked upon with great suspicion.

Alcohol is the usual reason for the police to demand early kick-off times. But to change a kick-off time for this reason is as ineffective as banning alcohol altogether before a game. During the 1998 World Cup in France I was caught up in an incident that was a direct result of this paranoia. England were playing Columbia in the small industrial town of Lens. The authorities insisted that every bar was to be closed as alcohol could cause fans to start trouble. There's nothing special about the town of Lens (let's think of it as the Swindon of France) and there's not much else to do there other than sit in a bar or a restaurant.

With virtually the whole town closed, thousands of England fans were left walking around getting bored. I ended up sitting near a large roundabout with a few hundred other England fans. A couple of supporters had walked into the road and draped St George Cross flags over moving cars. As a result the police moved in with serious intent towards everyone who was in the area. Within seconds I and other England fans who had done nothing wrong were being chased down a tunnel by a massive mob of baton-wielding riot police. We spent the next five hours penned into an area so that we couldn't even leave the town. This alcohol ban was later described by British politicians, who were not in Lens, as a great success and an effective way of stopping football-related trouble. All that tells me is that the people who make laws for our benefit and apparent health and safety actually have no idea about the reality of these situations. And that includes the police who should not have the right to dictate the time a football match is played. If the police had their way then no event would ever be allowed to happen just in case somebody might actually want to attend it.

By 2006 an average of four out of ten Premiership fixtures did not kick off at the traditional 3:00pm on a Saturday afternoon. During the 2006-07 season Liverpool's first seven Premiership games kicked off at times other than 3.00pm.[3] Football is now played every day of the week and irregular kick-off times prioritise the TV viewer ahead of the supporter who attends the matches. Sky and Setanta, by law, cannot broadcast a live match at 3.00pm on a Saturday. But even if live football were allowed to be shown on TV at this time there would still be the same amount of live games on at midday. In the 2005-06 season, Manchester City and Everton kicked off on a Sunday at 11.30am for a Premiership fixture. This was to accommodate Sky television coverage as they tried to cram in as many live games as they could do on that

---

[3] The 2006-07 season began on August 19th. Liverpool's first Saturday 3.00pm fixture wasn't until October 14th.

Sunday. A lot of people are still in a deep sleep at 11.30am on a Sunday, let alone in any mood to go to a football match.

The right time to play a game on a weekend 3.00pm. It's after lunchtime and it gives fans the early afternoon to relax and get ready to go to the game. Most people work hard Monday to Friday and prefer a longer lie in bed on a Saturday morning. Yet for away fans who follow their teams up and down the country a 12.45pm kick-off will normally mean that they would have to wake up earlier than they would do for a work day. TV companies will schedule a game at this time between two teams located at different ends of the country. Fans of London clubs are expected to travel to places like Newcastle for a game that kicks off at 5.15pm. By the time the game ends there are no more trains heading back to London until the following day. Of course the same thing applies when Newcastle play in London at irregular times. In 2003 Newcastle United played at Arsenal on a Friday night for a Premiership fixture. Many fans travelling from Newcastle for that game must have spent over £200 on rail fares, match tickets, and overnight accommodation in London etc.

In general, Friday is the one day of the week that doesn't feature heavily in the football calendar. It's actually a great time to go and watch a football match. It is at the start of the weekend and there is a good vibrant atmosphere. Maybe the Monday night live match should become the Friday night live match? Either way, the important thing to remember, is that in order to accommodate television coverage, a game from the weekend moves to a weekday. Therefore travelling fans should be more thoughtfully considered, and these games should feature teams in close proximity to one another (I'm not advocating more than a couple of games a season for each club on a Friday night, some of us do have social lives outside football). With modern day fixture lists, the fans who attend every match must take a very large percentage of their annual holiday leave just to follow their football team each season.

If away fans didn't attend these fixtures then the TV companies would have a product that is less saleable to the viewer, and the football clubs would also lose out on gate receipts. If that were to happen you can be sure that things would change very quickly. The TV companies and the football clubs have shown a terrible lack of respect for the attending fan and for this they should be met with a lack of respect in return.

Chelsea FC and billionaire takeovers

"We realise you [Liverpool owners George Gillet and Tom Hicks] are only here for the profits, that you perceive Liverpool as an ATM shaped like a stadium... Tread carefully. Liverpool are not a mere business, English football clubs are not about bucks and mortar; when fans gather they don't talk about bottom lines but about shared heartaches and triumphs. "

Henry Winter – Daily Telegraph 2007

Q: According to Wikipedia, which of the following five allegations do Manchester City owner and ex-President of Thailand Thaksin Shinawatra have labelled against him?

      (a) Human rights abuses
      (b) Conflicts of interest
      (c) Hostility towards a free press
      (d) Treason
      (e) Demagogy and dictatorship

A: All of them. Welcome to the English Premiership Mr Shinawatra, we're sure you'll find it to your taste and satisfaction.

In 2006-07, it was the period of the foreign takeover in the Premiership. West Ham, Portsmouth, Aston Villa, Liverpool and Manchester City were all bought out by foreign investors in a trend that is unlikely to fall out of fashion. Three of our biggest clubs alone – Aston Villa, Manchester United and Liverpool have been taken over by American tycoons since 2005. One thing that every club in the Premiership now has in common is that they have to find some way to compete on a level playing field with a club in West London whose spending power since 2003 has dramatically upset the financial balance of English football.

In my old secondary school in North London the number of pupils was usually around the 1,000 mark. Football was the most popular sport and the best supported team was Tottenham, the area where most of the kids came from. The only other teams that anyone supported in that school were Liverpool and Arsenal. Throughout my five years in the school there was only ever one Chelsea fan and not one Manchester United fan. Everyone respected the Chelsea fan because he followed a team that were not fashionable and who played poor football. He got the piss taken out of him as well, but it didn't matter because he attended every Chelsea home game and people respected his loyalty. In those days a Chelsea fan in North London was as common as a Greek vegetarian. Times have changed and there are now legions of blue shirts in every borough of the capital and beyond. The Chelsea fans who now populate the schools throughout England might be able to gloat to their friends about their team's glory. But whether or not their friends respect them for who they've chosen to support is another matter.

Having been bankrolled by a billionaire, Chelsea have achieved great success on the football field, but respect for their achievements is something that has no doubt been lacking. Money can't always buy respect or happiness, and I've not seen a manager look so unhappy after his team had just won the English championship trophy as Jose Mourinho did at the end of the 2005-06 season. He was upset because never has a championship winning team been greeted with such disinterest and apathy as it was that year. On the same day that Chelsea clinched the title, all the headlines went to Portsmouth FC who in the same afternoon avoided relegation. Mourinho, clearly upset by this, felt that all season his team never got the credit they deserved by neutral fans and the media, and he chucked his championship winner's medal into the crowd in anger.

Usually great teams are hated but at the same time they tend to be respected: teams such as Liverpool in the 1980s, the Manchester United sides in the 1990s, and various different Arsenal teams under Arsene Wenger and George Graham. With Chelsea, that respect has been lacking and that's because people believe that their success has come about solely through money. Chelsea fans like to deny that it's all about money and claim that the reason they have achieved success on the field is because they had the best manager. Yet money buys a great manager, as Mourinho would probably not have gone to Chelsea in 2004 without the prospect of an open chequebook. To deny that Chelsea's success is not just down to the money is a fantasy. Before the Abramovich takeover Chelsea had only ever won the league once in their whole history. Within just three years of unlimited Russian oil money being pumped into the club, they had won two more!

Chelsea are the USA of the football world for the following five reasons:

1. Not much history.
2. More money than everyone else.
3. An arrogant bully-boy mentality and superiority complex.

4. Always crying about the fact that nobody likes them.

5. The bombing of Iraq.

Okay I made that last one up. It's obvious that I'm biased. I don't like Chelsea very much and never have done, even during the 1980s when Ken Bates bought them for less than the price of a pint of beer. I am trying to be objective and I'm not having a pop at Chelsea simply because I don't like them. It's easy to criticise the Blues but let's be honest about the culture of Premiership football before the days of Roman Abramovich and his billions. When Abramovich took over at Chelsea in 2003 all of the following six things were commonplace in football.

1. Obscene player wages

2. Crazy transfer fees.

3. Overbearing advertising.

4. Corporate priorities.

5. Uncompetitive English league.

6. Clive Tyldesley.

So the same problems that are currently in football were already in place back in 2003. Chelsea alone cannot be blamed for ruining football, but they have provided the final nails in the coffin. What Abramovich's billions have done is raise the bar even further at a time when football needed to be less dominated by money. It needed to go back in the other direction, but instead football has become even more obsessed with making vast profits. This is because the rival clubs have to try and compete on a level playing field with Chelsea. Other clubs justify high ticket prices and any other way to make money on the grounds that they have to compete with the spending power of the Blues. But the scary thing is that no matter how much revenue most of the other clubs make, they will never be equal to Chelsea on a financial level.

Roman Abramovich is the eleventh richest man on the planet and the second richest man in the UK. His wealth is estimated at around $18.2 billion. In early 2007 Liverpool were on the verge of being bought out by Sheikh Mohammed bin Rashid Al Maktoum, the ruler of the UAE. Maktoum is thought to be the fifth richest man alive and worth £27 billion (there is debate as to whether half of that fortune actually belongs to him or the state). The deal fell through, but had Maktoum taken over Liverpool, then his money could very well have done for them what the wealth of Abramovich has done for Chelsea. But for football as a whole the takeover would have been damaging because of the wealth gap that is already widening between a handful of clubs and everyone else. There is no possible way that the smaller clubs can compete with such market dominance, and we are seeing a financial hierarchy that is taking away the dreams of those who have the ambition but not the spending power. Liverpool's new American owners George Gillett and Tom Hicks do not have the billions of Abramovich or Maktoum, but they still have the power to position Liverpool near the top of that financial hierarchy in Europe.

The big question is whether or not the foreign businessmen who are buying out our football clubs are prepared to invest more money into the club than they get back. These new investors in football are unlikely to be modern equivalents of Jack Walker (with the exception of Roman Abramovich). Jack Walker was a man who in the 1990s poured money into Blackburn Rovers because he wanted to see the team win trophies. He didn't do it for financial gain, he did it because he loved Blackburn Rovers. He put far more money into the club than he was ever to get back. When George Gillet refers to Liverpool FC as a 'franchise', it gives out the impression that he sees the club primarily as a business venture. If a billionaire comes to Arsenal and actually moves the club away from corporate branding and lowers ticket prices, whilst at the same time investing in the team, then I will welcome that person with open arms. But if the new wealthy investors of other clubs are anything to go by, then this is not very likely to happen.

Defenders of these people claim that football's new investors are sporting enthusiasts who are not in it for the money. Okay, so why are these so-called 'sporting enthusiasts' not buying up world famous clubs in Brazil and Argentina? Easy answer, those teams don't make enough money. They want a piece of the Premiership pie because the annual revenue of the Premier League clubs is so much higher than any other football league. Fans don't appear to benefit from these takeovers, and the more money that comes into the game just ends up being spent on higher transfer fees and fatter contracts for the players. Roman Abramovich has lost money by investing in Chelsea FC (directly anyway, it is widely thought his status as Chelsea owner makes him more money in other areas). In fairness to Abramovich, he does appear to be very passionate about football. He attends most games which is more than can be said for someone like Malcolm Glazer (has Glazer even been to a game?). It's claimed that after Chelsea lost a semi-final in the Champions League, Abramovich was in the team dressing room crying his eyes out. But that doesn't hide the fact that the financial dominance of a few is a clear negative on the competitive nature of the English Premiership. Without a decent level of competitiveness there can be no real excitement or drama. UEFA have recognized this problem and in late 2006 it was reported that they would be looking into bringing in laws that would prevent a club spending money in a way that is out of proportion with their annual revenue. If these laws ever do go forward and get passed by the European Union, then the days of a club like Chelsea being bankrolled to success by a billionaire could be coming to an end.

Ticket pricing

I went to a West End cinema the other day to see the latest blockbuster movie. It is arguably the best cinema in the whole country. Great sound, giant screen, nice seats, impressive art deco surroundings. The ticket wasn't cheap – £13.50. I suppose that is quite a lot of money just to watch a film. Then again, I could have paid £20 for the cheapest seat at Leyton Orient. Cold weather, uncomfortable plastic seats, lower division football.

The issue of high ticket pricing is without doubt one of the key factors in the death of the people's game, and the clearest manifestation of the big con. This whole issue will be featured in Chapter six. The question is simple – does the price we now pay for football represent value for money?

Cautions and petty laws

In recent years the game has moved on rapidly, generally for the better. More games are televised, more money is spent, more games are played, even more laws are introduced. In fact so much change has occurred that sometimes I think we are getting away from what the thirteen original laws assume, that to play football all you need is honesty, courage and skill.

Sir Bobby Charlton

When I was a teenager I used to play football at New River Astro Turf pitch in Haringey with friends from school. One day to all our surprise we saw a true football legend heading a coaching session for youngsters on this same pitch. That legend was Sir Bobby Charlton. He saw us all gawping at him and he walked over to us for a chat. We were all starstruck and hardly said a word to him, but he was very friendly. He told us that when he was a player he went his whole career without receiving one yellow card and that we should try and follow the same example.

Another high profile player never to have received a yellow card was Gary Lineker, who retired in the early 1990s. From the same era, England striker Alan Smith finished his career with just the one yellow card to his name. For an honest player to do the same today is almost impossible. It could only be achieved if a player went a whole career without making a tackle, without showing emotion and, more importantly, never actually playing a game.

It seems now, that a player can earn a yellow card for simply breathing in a funny way, or for not shaving. A red card used to be a headline and even a yellow card was greeted with excitement from the TV commentator. Now most red cards appear to come about through two yellow cards for two minor offences. The number of yellow cards issued is also not helped by the poor sportsmanship of players who con the referee into giving free kicks. It's particularly annoying to see the players themselves encouraging referees to hand out cautions by waving their hand in the air and pretending to hold a yellow card. That is a gesture that actually should warrant a yellow card, yet always goes unpunished.

The 2006 World Cup saw the record number of red cards and this record was broken as early as the second round of the competition. It's sad to see a player miss out on a major final because of yellow cards received in earlier rounds in the competition. The World Cup final is the pinnacle for every professional footballer, and to be denied this pinnacle because of something so petty is unfair. This was highlighted in the 1990 World Cup semi-final when Paul Gascoigne received a yellow card against Germany after a mistimed tackle and a bit of injury feigning from the German player. It was Gascoigne's second yellow card of the tournament and had England reached the final,

Gascoigne would have been suspended. His reaction to receiving the yellow card became iconic as he cried his eyes out in the knowledge that he would miss out on the chance to play in what would have been the biggest game of his life in the prime of his career. In 2006 Frenchman Louis Saha was suspended from the World Cup Final because of a yellow card received in the semi-final for a fair tackle. Because yellow cards are now so common in tournaments a player should have to receive at least one a game to warrant a suspension for a final.

It's unfair to just blame referees for the amount of yellow and red cards handed out in the modern game, because they can only implement the laws that they are given. People in football demand both common sense and consistency from the referees, but for a referee to apply both is very difficult. Let's look at two scenarios that both warrant a red card, and see whether or not consistency and common sense can both be applied.

When the last defender, brings down an attacking player, modern laws dictate that he has to be issued with a red card...

1. Goalkeeper A, who is the last defender, runs out of the 25 yard box and deliberately fouls the attacker. The goalkeeper is sent off, and a free-kick is awarded outside the 25 yard box. From the resulting free-kick the ball goes wide of the goal.

2. Goalkeeper B, who is the last defender, brings down the attacker, without intent, inside the 25 yard box. The goalkeeper is sent off, and a penalty-kick is awarded. A goal is scored from the resulting penalty-kick.

By being consistent, and by strictly applying the laws of the game, the referee must produce a red card on both these occasions. By using common sense, the referee can feel satisfied that goalkeeper B made an honest attempt for the ball, and that the penalty-kick alone is sufficient punishment for the foul.

The football authorities have gone too far in making football a non-contact game. It is far easier to give away a foul than it used to be, and the merest of contact can result in a free-kick. In fairness, there was a need to give skilful players more protection from being fouled out of the game. The most notable example of this was in the 1982 World Cup when Diego Maradona was kicked and fouled constantly by players who would get away with this tactic unpunished. This limited Maradona's game and no matter how good a player he was, there was nothing he could do when every time he got the ball he was being physically assaulted. A similar fate happened to Pele when he was kicked out of the 1966 World Cup by aggressive European opposition.

There was a need for stricter rules in favour of protection, but it's now swung too much in the other direction and players are being penalised for making non-dangerous genuine attempts at tackles. Games are being ruined because on too many occasions a player is sent off early in the match. These laws are cheating the paying spectator and it's unfair on the managers and the players who fall victim to these decisions. Instead of handing out yellow cards for genuine attempts at a tackle, there should be more yellow cards for things like dissent towards the officials, time wasting, diving and feigning injury. However, the lawmakers seem more concerned with punishing players for trivial matters such as removing their shirt, or celebrating a goal too close to the crowd. The football authorities are paranoid about any display of emotion that might get a crowd up from their plastic seats and they want to punish players for anything that might encourage this.

Midway though the 2006 World Cup, FIFA president Sepp Blatter accused the England team of being boring en route to reaching the quarter finals. This was rich to say the least because if there's one man on earth who's responsible for making football boring, then it's Sepp Blatter. He's the head of an organisation that has implemented laws which have taken away the competitive edge from football and harmed the flow of a match. If the referee blowing the whistle and stopping the play so many times during a match is supposed to favour attacking play and make the game more exciting, then it has failed. Sepp Blatter should look back to the 1982 World Cup when Maradona was kicked out of the tournament because, despite some bad tackles, that tournament was arguably the greatest World Cup of all time, and was better and more real than the watered-down product that he now provides us with. As fans we want to see the best players protected, but we also want to see a side of the game that doesn't penalise physical but fair play. This is all a long way from the days of 1860 when Lord Kinnard wrote a letter to Scottish team Queens Park before a match pleading "Please let's have hacking. It's such fun!"

Unfortunately the world has too many Sepp Blatters who have jobs in high up places. The laws in football are forever being meddled with and the problem with these lawmakers is that they're of the same mould as the kind of people who work in health and safety and risk assessment. Their job is never done and they have to find a fault with something resulting in more bureaucracy. This kind of obsession is turning football and more importantly the world into a bureaucrat's paradise. A paradise that has red tape round the edge of the island just in case someone wants to go for a swim and risk drowning. The general public are treated like children as the health and safety brigade find new ways to protect us from ourselves. During the 2005 Trafalgar anniversary, the man who was acting the part of the fearless Lord Nelson was made to wear a life jacket as he made his way down the River Thames! It's fair to say that this re-enactment didn't look very authentic. My brother works in a school and was berated for walking down a corridor with an empty tea mug as it was deemed a health and safety hazard. This is all as crazy as the football lawmakers who believe that a player who removes his shirt could incite a crowd to riot.

In 2007 the Football League proposed an idea in which regular league games that end in draws would be concluded by a penalty shoot-out. The motive behind this idea would be to make the game more exciting (even though it would actually encourage more defensive play from weaker teams who would play for the draw), but football became the most popular sport in the world for what it is, and doesn't need to keep on being changed.

Of all the stupid laws in football the icing on the cake is the law that is enforced when a player gets up from being on the ground injured. In the years gone by there was a simple way to deal with this problem. Once the player got up from the ground after recovering from a knock, the player simply played on. Not anymore. That was too simple, and therefore had to be dealt with by the men in suits who've probably never even kicked a ball before, but apparently understand the game better than anyone. Now once a player gets up from being injured he must walk off the pitch. Once he's off the pitch he must get waved back on by the referee. Why? I don't know. Nobody knows other than the people who came up with this strange law. What will they think of next? Maybe the player should have to send a text message to the referee for permission to re-enter the pitch – the excuse being that the referee needs to be sure that the player still has all his senses after being fouled (each player could be sponsored by a phone company which would bring more revenue into the game, thus making football a better product). I'd better stop this piece now before I give ideas to anyone at FIFA and T-Mobile. Let's move on…

The new consumer

"The stadium is where Argentineans go to let off steam. Football belongs to simple players and poor people. These are people who for example can't afford to go to the opera. So they go to Boca [Juniors] or River [Plate] and that fuels the flames and their anger."

Diego Maradona

Before the World Cup in 2006, the BBC aired a programme in which Gary Lineker travelled to Argentina to meet Diego Maradona. The programme featured Maradona attending a game at Boca Juniors, a club located in the docklands of Buenos Aires. It's the club in which he started his career and where he is now considered an honorary president and is worshipped by the fans as a god. Boca are one of the biggest clubs in the world and have a fanatical partisan support that is unrivalled in football. Maradona attends every game in his Boca shirt and watches the games with his family from his own outdoor executive box. The BBC documentary showed Maradona to be as passionate a supporter as he was a player. He couldn't sit still for one second and looked to have spent the whole game on his feet shouting, hanging over the edge of the balcony of the executive box, singing, dancing and generally loving the experience of being at a football match. The greatest player the world has ever seen shows more passion as a football spectator than the majority of fans who now attend games in the English Premiership. Some people say that a football team would not function with eleven Peles or eleven Maradonas (I personally think that's bollocks!). Whether that be the case or not, I do know that if every stadium had 40,000 Maradonas in the crowd then no football match would ever be boring.

After the issue of ticket pricing the reason I don't attend many football matches anymore is because of the lack of passion from the crowd, and the detachment that comes with that. The support shown by football fans in other countries is off the chart in comparison with English supporters. But then English fans still hold this reputation as being the most passionate supporters in the world. In one sense we are, as English supporters are loyal in terms of attendance. We stick with our teams through the bad times. Lower division games in England can produce crowds of 30,000 or more which is very rare in other countries. And what can be more passionate and dedicated than a Torquay United fan who travels up to Carlisle for a mid-table match on a Tuesday night in winter? I would never criticise these fans who keep their teams alive through their loyalty. But what I don't understand is the apathy shown by supporters of teams who play the best football. It seems that the better football a team plays the more likely the fans are to leave the stadium before the end of the game. At certain grounds, one third of the stadium can be empty by the eighty-ninth minute. This is because the type of 'supporter' that now attends football is more concerned about an easier journey home in their Mercedes 4x4, than witnessing what could potentially be the most dramatic part of the game.

There are no English crowds who create anything like the kind of spectacle as say Boca Juniors or other domestic teams from countries like Brazil, Holland, Italy, Germany, France, Greece, Croatia etc. The South American and European football fans can create a dramatic cauldron-like atmosphere with flags flying and flares smoking, and in this respect they put the English fans to shame. When I've been to some of these countries and attended a game, the noise and colour that is generated from the stands has been simply breathtaking.

This type of passion is not to be confused with hooliganism and violence. It is also true that in recent years there has been much more football-related crowd trouble in other countries than in England. But in the English league, the measures to stop crowd trouble have gone from an attitude of apathy in the 1970s and 1980s to an attitude of paranoia and draconian laws in the present day. The attitude in Europe over the past decade has been similar to that of England in the 1970s and 1980s, and more should be done in these countries to prevent this sort of hooliganism. After an Italian policeman was killed by fans in Sicily during a Palermo game in 2007, the publicity highlighted a problem that has become far worse in mainland Europe than in England – the country which many Europeans have looked down upon as being the masters of hooliganism.

A month before the Sicily incident, Feyenoord from Holland had been thrown out of European competition due to crowd violence, and the general consensus has been that hooliganism is out of control throughout the continent. The irony is that some countries in Europe (particularly Italy) are now likely to be looking towards England as an example of how to re-brand the game and sell it to a new consumer. During this time of rising crowd trouble in Europe, and particularly after the death of the policeman in Sicily, there has been a lot of backslapping by pundits in England along with clichés like "it just shows you how far this country's come when you look at the trouble you now get abroad."

But the authorities in European football should not look at the English model as the perfect example of fan culture, because the exuberance from the crowd has reversed too far in the other direction. In this day and age in English football stadiums, I get shouted at by other supporters to 'sit down' if I dare to stand up in excitement when my team has a goal-scoring opportunity. The last game at which this happened was during a North London derby between Arsenal and Spurs – a game which is sold on the basis of being a 'highly charged affair'. So 'highly charged' that I can't even get up from my seat when I think that my team might score a goal! Despite the occasional bit of crowd trouble from a minority of fans in other countries, the atmosphere and sense of freedom in these stadiums makes you feel alive and part of something special. In contrast when I attend English football matches nowadays the whole environment sometimes makes me feel like I'm part of a glorified graveyard.

The atmosphere in English grounds has unquestionably been nullified due to the authorities and their never-ending restrictions, but ultimately passion comes down to the supporters themselves. The club I support has the reputation for having quiet fans, hence the old phrase 'Highbury the library'. But in truth the Arsenal fans are no less passionate than fans of most other clubs in England. I've been to grounds all over the country and seen no better. The roar at St. James Park was little more than a whimper. The Chelsea crowd at Stamford Bridge would cause no disturbance to a cinema audience. The 'Theatre of Dreams' at Old Trafford is in reality more in line with the title of this book. One set of fans who do deserve to be singled out for great support towards their team are supporters of Portsmouth FC. Win, lose or draw the Pompy fans support their team with great passion and belief. This positive attitude from their fans was regarded as one of the reasons that Portsmouth FC managed to avoid relegation in the 2005-06 season. Confidence is crucial to success in football and nothing can give a player more confidence than a crowd that is encouraging and gets behind the team.

When I sit amongst a crowd that shows no passion I long to be somewhere else. The supporters who do try to make some noise end up as lone voices and even get given funny looks by other fans. People pay good money to sit down and be entertained, but my argument is that without passion there can be no great drama. The same principle applies to something like music. The best concerts I've been to have been the ones where the crowd complement the performers. However, I've noticed that in recent years, crowds at music gigs have also become more timid and are now spectators rather than a vital part of the entertainment. If being amongst a boring football crowd is frustrating, then being amongst a similar crowd at, for example, a rock gig is just downright depressing. It's as if the whole of society has had the life sucked out of it, and has lost the ability to let off steam (other than the morons who let off steam by acting like aggressive drunken yobs, though maybe their behaviour is a result of that lost energy at football matches, music gigs etc?).

One explanation for this could be our TV culture. People are so used to watching entertainment on their TV screens that when they attend an event they simply stand still with their arms folded and wait to be entertained. So many people at events now also seem to spend the whole time recording the match/concert on their mobile phone rather than experiencing with their own eyes what's in front of them. I reckon they're of the same mould as tourists who spend so much time behind a video camera that they only see the landmarks they visited on the home video of their holiday. I will never forget an image I saw in a newspaper in 2005 that showed Pope John Paul being taken through St Peter's Square in an open coffin, and the amount of people who were looking at him only through the screen of their mobile phone or video camera.

A lot of the people who make up football and music crowds today are the ones who should be at home in front of their TV screens. But the problem is that these are the people with the money and the contacts, and in modern day entertainment that's more important than anything. I'll give you an example of the kind of people who have these contacts and just why some events don't generate the kind of excitement from the crowd that the occasion warrants. One night in 2003 I had to cover for my sister on a house-sitting job for a couple who had tickets to see the Rolling Stones at Wembley Arena. I had actually tried to buy tickets for this gig myself but was quoted £180 a ticket by Wembley Arena. I would have liked to have seen the Rolling Stones play live, but for that price I would have expected to have had Jade Jagger sitting on my lap. I wasn't that surprised when the couple told me that their tickets came about through work and that they hadn't had to pay for them. I'd spoken to a few other people who had attended that

Rolling Stones tour and none of them had paid money for their tickets. No wonder then that those who do actually pay for tickets pay well over the odds. When tour organisers boast that a concert has sold out in just twenty minutes then it's probably because only twenty tickets got sold to the general public. I had only been house-sitting for around two and a half hours when the couple returned home. The timing seemed odd and I asked them if the concert had been cancelled. It turned out that they left the gig an hour early in order to beat the traffic – WHAT! These guys left a Rolling Stones concert an hour early because they wanted an easier ride home from one part of North London to the other!! Why didn't they just give me the tickets? Problem solved. I and a friend could have seen the Rolling Stones and had a memorable night, whilst this couple could have simply stayed at home. A crowd of this sort is unappreciative, spoilt and think of themselves as too important to show any sort of emotion, whilst real passion goes to waste on the outside.

There's no doubt that football crowds have changed in recent years in both wealth and gender. Some people blame the increased number of women at football matches for the lack of atmosphere, but I don't think that's the case at all.

The vast majority of spectators in stadiums are still male so why put the blame on a minority of women? It's true that you do get some women at matches who look bored and would really rather be shopping instead. But that is counter-balanced by the amount of men at football grounds who are as unenthusiastic as the girlfriends whom they have dragged along. And I know plenty of women who are far more knowledgeable and passionate about football than a lot of male football fans. Many women follow lower league clubs whilst many men have no loyalty and support whoever they think is the best team. Football is now considered family entertainment, and I think it's great that the game is now supposedly a more suitable environment for women and children (although having said that I always felt comfortable and safe at football stadiums when I was a kid). But football being a family game is just one side of things. The other side includes young men who have energy to burn, and who will create the atmosphere in the stadiums. The truth is that without us the atmosphere is dead, and we shouldn't simply be dismissed and told that we have to sit down and be quiet. After all, football was originally founded on the very basis of young people letting off steam. There are many reasons why football crowds have become more timid over recent years, but the main reasons are stewarding and security, and all-seater stadiums. Let's start with our friends in the orange bibs.

Stewarding and security

Gone are the days when we would see rival fans engage in full scale battles on the field of play as in the 1970s and 1980s. Other than nostalgic football thugs, most people would agree that this is a good thing, and that better and well managed crowd control has played a part in that change. However when fans are threatened with eviction if they even dare to wave around fake twenty pound notes with Ashley Cole's face on it – then some might just argue that football needs to be a lot less authoritarian in the way it treats its most important people. Before a Chelsea v Arsenal game in the 2006-07 season, it was reported that any fan caught with one of these fake notes that was mimicking Cole risked eviction from Stamford Bridge, for the crime of incitement. It would now appear that hurting the feelings of a £90,000 a week superstar is deemed worthy of being thrown out from a football ground.

The character Winston Smith from George Orwell's *Nineteen Eighty Four* would not feel out of place in a football stadium these days. The camera surveillance is as overbearing as in the rest of our country, which is the CCTV capital of the world. Football stadiums are now very restricted environments where everyone must conform to the strict rules or face eviction from the ground. Very much like most nightclubs, which pretend to be places where people can lose themselves but are actually the very opposite. Every year the football authorities find new things to ban and confiscate. At Upton Park in 2005 I witnessed a senior steward try to confiscate somebody's mobile phone just because that person took a photo of the game. If a fan has paid good money for a ticket should they not have the right to take a photograph of themselves at the game from their mobile phone? Are the club worried that people are taking these photographs in order to sell them? It's not as if these pictures would be sold to the sports pages of the Sunday newspapers. You don't tend to see too many professional sports photographers using Nokias or Sony Eriksons for that back page snap.

The list of banned items from football grounds ranges from the sensible to the ridiculous. Banning things like Stanley knives and beer bottles probably does make sense. But the traditional flag is now banned from many grounds as the bamboo flag pole is now perceived as a weapon. I can see where they're coming from as the flagpole does have a troubled history. In 1945 President Truman had to contemplate dropping flagpoles on Japanese cities in order to bring an end to the Second World War. A bamboo stick with a piece of cloth attached to it reading 'FA CUP WINNERS' wiped out the entire city of Hiroshima in seconds. Other weapons of mass destruction that have needed to be dealt with at football grounds include the dreaded bell. I've seen a Portsmouth fan get ejected from Highbury for standing up and ringing this deadly killing machine in support of his team. The other Portsmouth fans were unhappy at the stewards for this harsh treatment towards one of their fans. However they have to realise that this bell could have suddenly flown out of the man's hand and sliced off the head of a nearby spectator. Health and safety must take first priority, and without this type of enforcement we would never have heard the 'YOU'RE NOT RINGING ANYMORE' chant directed at the Pompey fan as he was led out of the stadium.

The nearest I've come to being ejected from a football stadium by stewards was at Hull City in 1998. A group of us had committed the offence of singing 'YOU'RE SHIT AND YOU KNOW YOU ARE' at the home team, which is a chant heard regularly at football grounds all over the country. At Hull City though we were confronted by the head steward who told us that under the new football act, swearing is an offence at football grounds and that we would be ejected if we didn't stop it. My cousin informed him that the word 'shit' is in the English dictionary and that we were merely making an observation towards the style of football being played by the home team. The steward didn't buy that excuse and sounded like a policeman with his "I'm not prepared to argue" stance.

I haven't got a problem with the majority of people who do stewarding. Most are there to do a day's work and are not on a power trip. The money they get paid is peanuts and some companies that employ stewards take advantage of them. Many stewards will be expected to work six hours for an event, yet they will only get paid for five hours. This is because they are told that the first hour they work is 'preparation'. Is preparation not part of a day's work? In 2005 I very briefly worked for a stewarding and security firm that operated in this way, though I refused to work for them at football matches. I was with this firm so that I could occasionally work at events that I wanted to see but couldn't get tickets for, such as rock gigs or a day at the races. Even so, I was still expected to go through an induction that qualified me to work at football grounds. The induction was an education in paranoia and it showed me just how much ordinary football fans are viewed with suspicion. Every fan is under surveillance and every fan is considered a potential 'breach of the peace'.

In my experience with this firm, the people I disliked were not the ordinary stewards but some of the steward supervisors and senior stewards. These are the people at football grounds who I feel are both over-zealous and get off on power trips. In the 2006-07 season, Reading goalkeeper Marcus Hahnerman had a ritual of giving away his keeper's jersey to a lucky fan after the game. It was a simple way of thanking people for their support, and is the kind of gesture that the supporters always appreciate. But when approaching his own fans with his jersey after a match at Sheffield United, Hahnerman found himself surrounded by ten stewards who refused to allow him anywhere near the Reading supporters. Naturally Hahnerman was frustrated by the unnecessary interfering from the Sheffield United stewards and ended up in a verbal confrontation. The head of security at Sheffield United justified the behaviour from his staff by using the tiresome health and safety and risk assessment excuse. He claimed there was a risk of people getting crushed by a surge forward by eager fans wanting to get their hands on the souvenir. When listening to this sort of wisdom it's quite amazing to think that performers over the years have thrown souvenirs to their audience without creating mass scenes of death and carnage. Back to the real world and it is a sad and pathetic state of affairs when security and stewarding has become so paranoid and aggressive, a player cannot even approach a fan to hand over a gift. The most over-zealous and aggressive display of stewarding I've ever witnessed was at Ipswich Town in 2001. Dennis Bergkamp had narrowly missed a goal-scoring chance that would have won Arsenal the game in the last minute of the match. A fan in the front row thought that Bergkamp had scored and he jumped out of his seat and over an advertising hoarding which was a couple of yards from where he was sitting. He soon realised that his excitement had taken him into an area of the stadium that was restricted, and he quickly got back into his seat. Within seconds about ten gorillas in orange bibs were on top of him before he was roughly dragged out of the stadium. The way the stewards jumped on him you would have thought that he was a sniper about to shoot the president – not a football fan who thought his team had just scored a winning goal in the last minute. The Ipswich stewards were like predators jumping on top of their prey, and from their expressions it was obvious that they relished imposing their authority. All a situation like that needed was a steward to have a quick word with the fan and to explain that jumping over the hoardings is not allowed. The fan involved in this incident is likely to have received a fine and a banning order from football.

What's annoying about the attitude of some stewards is the way they think have the right to order people about in an environment totally out of their jurisdiction. For example in 2004 I ended up having an argument with a ticket seller at the box office at Arsenal. I had been queuing for tickets since 7:00am. It was a horrible rainy morning and after a couple of hours I had made it to the front of the queue. My membership details were unfairly questioned and I was refused tickets and treated with disdain by the man at the box office.[4] Feeling wet, tired and pissed off I then felt it appropriate to tell the man at the box office to "Go fuck yourself" as I was walking off. As I said this I then had a steward rush up and raise his voice at me. What right did this steward think he had to tell me how I should behave on a public street? The box office at Highbury was on the street not in the stadium. What did he think he was going to do? Chuck me off the street into the stadium? Ban me from the street for life?

All this enforcement at football matches makes fans feel like children under the eye of a teacher. Unfortunately most supporters seem docile enough to accept this part of the game. In my opinion any steward at a football match who is over-zealous and on a

---

[4] For the record, this incident was the straw that broke the camel's back. On that rainy day, I decided once and for all that my custom was not appreciated, and that's when I decided to stop attending football matches on a regular basis.

power trip should be singled out by the crowd and undermined throughout the rest of the game. At Upton Park the senior steward who tried to take away the camera phone of a fan spent the rest of the game having chants directed at him, and his snarling red face was a picture as the fans mocked him. In fact, I would have taken a picture of his face if it wasn't illegal.

All-seater stadiums

In 2007, the internet survey group the Football Fans Census asked 2,000 supporters if they would prefer to stand on the terraces and pay less. 74% said yes.

I'm not insensitive to the reasons why we now have all-seater stadiums. In 1989, 96 people died on a terrace at Hillsborough. In 1985, 37 people died on a terrace in the Heysel stadium in Brussels. But the reality is that at Hillsborough people died through under-investment, bad organisation, police errors and the steel fences which had more place in a zoo than a sporting arena. In Brussels in 1985, the Heysell stadium was not fit to hold any crowd let alone a crowd for a European Cup Final. After the Hillsborough disaster Lord Justice Taylor outlined a law which meant that every top flight football ground in England had to be all-seater. The terraces were to be no more. I think that Lord Justice Taylor probably came to this conclusion with the best of intentions and that he had the safety of football fans as his priority. I don't blame Lord Justice Taylor, but I think that he was wrong in his judgement. His report was an overreaction to the Hillsborough disaster and for this I blame the football clubs who under-invested in the fans and let the stadiums rot. Back in the 1980s some stadiums were in a pitiful state. A week before the Hillsborough tragedy a friend of mine had been to Millwall's old Cold Blow Lane stadium. At the time he made a comment that "One day someone's going to die at these stadiums." This comment was in reference to the facilities and nothing to do with Millwall fans. A week later a lot more than just one person died in the worst ever disaster in English football history. Back in the late 1980s these stadiums did need massive investment, but this could have incorporated terracing. Terraces can be clean, high tech and, more importantly, they can be safe. No disaster similar to Hillsborough could happen in a terrace that has better security monitoring, better exits, all-ticket games for big matches and, most importantly, no steel fences.

There can be no doubt that one of the main causes for high ticket pricing is the Taylor Report. As a young teenager when the Taylor Report came into effect I knew instantly that entrance to the grounds would be harder and more expensive due to reduced capacity. In the first few years of all-seater stadiums the change of ticket pricing wasn't that dramatic. However all-seater stadiums were soon to be met with modern-day player wage demands and agent greed. The new all-seater stands could not hold anywhere near the amount of spectators that the terraces were capable of. Highbury stadium at one time could hold 73,000 but after the Taylor report its capacity was reduced to only 38,000. English football stadiums in this modern era have never been bigger, but the crowd capacities have never been smaller. Charlton Athletics' Valley stadium was once the largest capacity league stadium in London, holding 75,000 due to one massive terrace that stretched from one end of the pitch to the other. Now the all-seater Valley only holds a mere 27,000. If stadiums such as St James Park, Eastlands and the Emirates had sections of terracing then the ground capacities would be near the 80,000 mark. If Old Trafford had sections of terracing then its capacity would be near 100,000. Think of the brand new 90,000 all-seater Wembley stadium, and what the capacity could be with sections of open terracing. With such high ground capacities, football would no longer be exclusive to those with money and would soon return to being a game for all the people. The current situation is one where thousands of people are locked out of football grounds each week because there are not enough seats available to meet the demand.

Many kids are brought up on a culture of watching their team play on TV rather than attending the live match, because they don't have the means or money to get hold of a ticket. That alone is enough of an argument to be able to claim that all-seater stadiums have been a negative influence on football. People talk about the comfort of all-seater stadiums, but most of these new stands lack space and I don't see what's so comfortable about having your knees crushed by the next row of seats. This bothers my knees and I'm only five foot seven inches! Sitting down in comfort is being at home on a sofa watching the TV or reading a book, so when did this become the main principle of attending a football match?

Contrary to modern belief, the terraces were fun. They were practical and more than anything they had a sense of freedom. You could choose where you wanted to stand and watch the game. Now we pay more money to sit down where someone tells us. In the old Arsenal stadium before it became all-seated, I would watch the games in the West Stand Junior Gunners section. In this terrace I would walk from one end of the pitch to the other. So whatever goal Arsenal were shooting towards I could stand at that end and get an excellent view of the goal my team were shooting at. Back then, if you didn't like the person you were positioned next to in the ground, you simply moved to another spot. Nowadays if we're stuck next to a person who offends us we have to put up with that annoyance for the whole game. In fact I have to admit that, being someone who regularly shouts and swears in football stadiums, I'm sure that I am that person who some people would rather move away from! But hey, don't blame me, blame Lord Justice Taylor and Mrs Thatcher. Terraces provided drama. Every time the opposition at Highbury scored I used to be mesmerised by the sight of the away fans' goal celebrations. It was electric. In the old terraces the goal celebrations would resemble a pack of bees swarming around together. It was a sea of people and the energy was breathtaking. But now, in this modern middle of the road all-seater environment, fans greet a goal by standing up, clapping for five seconds, and then sitting back down again. That release of energy is something that football has lost. I still feel like a young man, and I want to be on my feet at a time when I still have the energy and still have the knees.

The terraces at top level football were knocked down in the early 1990s when I was in my early teens and that was devastating for a young football fan who liked to bounce up and down. I think I felt more of a loss when the old North Bank terrace was bulldozed than I did when Arsenal left Highbury altogether in 2006. By that point Highbury was still a magical old stadium but an important part of its soul had been lost for well over a decade. The season after the North Bank terrace was demolished in 1992-93, the atmosphere in the ground had become so quiet the club tried to improve things by blaring out pre-recorded Arsenal chants through loudspeakers. That was a real low point in my time as a football fan, and even today it's clear that supporters have not properly adjusted to the culture of all-seater stadiums. I feel sorry for young football fans who will never get the chance to be part of that terrace culture and will never know just how special it was. So when people refer to the "bad old days of terracing" I find it ironic, because there are thousands of us who remember those days as being some of the best times of our lives.

In November 2005 Tony Blair was asked on BBC's *Football Focus* about the possibilities of bringing back terracing. He made it clear that it was a terrible idea and that he wasn't even prepared to even talk about the subject. A fine example of debate and democracy there from the man who was supposed to be the defender of our free speech. The likelihood of our current political leaders having a more favourable attitude towards terracing is also highly unlikely. But it's not just the politicians and football authorities that don't want to bring back terracing. Many fans have now grown used to the all-seater arrangement and would hate the thought of standing up at a football match. To those people who don't want to stand in a terrace and would rather sit down I say to them – fine. You sit, I'll stand. It's a simple arrangement, and one that was in place for well over one hundred years. Anyone who didn't want to stand on a terrace bought a seat. Yes, it really was that simple.

Football was more enjoyable when you could wake up on the day of the match and make a decision to go to the game. Fans now have the hassle of trying to buy tickets online or over the phone for a game that is weeks or even months away. At the very least clubs should give fans a section of the ground that is all-seater but where standing up is allowed. This is very common for many clubs in Europe who have allocated sections for their most partisan supporters. It's the perfect compromise in making football a suitable environment for both families and also for the more vocal supporters. When I attended a match at Juventus in 2006, the crowd was around the 50,000 mark, and it was spit up into two sections. Around 35,000 of the crowd watched the game sitting down, while the other 15,000 had their own section which was a spectacle of noise and colour. No club in England has this policy, and they're not likely to either because it doesn't fit in with their corporate image of the game. Any environment in which the fans have a sense of community is something the clubs would not want to encourage. When the fans have community they have organization, and when they have organization they have the power to change the way that football is run.

When a group of friends go to the cinema together they do not sit in separate seats in different sections of the cinema. When a party of people go to a restaurant they do not sit at separate tables and next to strangers. When football fans can't sit or stand together at a match, the game loses something right at the heart of its soul.

Overbearing advertising and marketing

"Oh by the way, if anyone in here works in advertising or marketing... kill yourself! No but seriously....do. Kill yourself. There's no rationalisation for what you do and you're Satan's little helpers. You're the ruiners of all things good. You're all thinking there's a joke coming here. There's not. This is not a joke. Kill yourselves. You are Satan's spawn filling the world with bile and garbage (large round of applause and cheers from the audience). You're fucking with us, kill yourselves. I know what all the marketing people are thinking right now. 'Bill's going for the anti marketing dollar. Hey that's a strong dollar, that's a good market.' God damn it I'm not doing that you scumbags. Stop putting a dollar sign on every fucking thing on the planet."

American stand-up comedian Bill Hicks – 1993.

Let me be the first to admit that I myself have made money out of football advertising. £250 to be exact, you see, back in 2004 I was Paul Scholes' body double for a Nike television commercial. Before you read on I must just clear up something very important. I'm NOT ginger. They dyed my hair and it took ten washes to get it out. To make matters worse Nike didn't even pay me for dyeing my hair as the production rules stated that I should only receive money for a haircut. Where's the justice in that? Shooting the commercial was great fun and it was an advert in which Thierry Henry was being chased around his house by other players contracted to Nike. No famous players were present unfortunately, just body doubles like myself.[5] The back of my head was seen in the advert as I chased Henry down a hallway along with several other United players. I'd love to know how much the real Paul Scholes earned for that advert. I've heard accusations from friends implying that it was me who deliberately missed the penalty kick for Manchester United against Arsenal in the 2005 FA Cup Final penalty shoot-out. It wasn't. That time it was the real Paul Scholes. Nike actually asked me to miss it for him but they were still unwilling to pay me for dyeing my hair ginger so I turned them down. Where's my agent!

This is not the sort of advertising that harms football. If companies such as Nike and Adidas want to pay millions to players then that's fine. Sponsors will only pay players who perform well and who are worth the money, so good luck to them. But what about a form of advertising that might affect a person's enjoyment of watching a game? What about the new digital advertising hoardings that are common throughout European football? Those who run the game were not content with motionless advertising hoardings, or ones that would occasionally flip between one advert to another.

They've imposed digital hoardings on us that flash adverts at fans throughout the whole match. They're trying to make the touchlines in football stadiums look like Times Square or the Las Vegas strip! The first club in England to have these installed was Manchester United, as always the pioneers of commercialism in football. These hoardings are an obscene and offensive imposition in modern football. They're obscene because they're so horribly effective. My eyes sub-consciously get taken away from the actual game and towards these flashing messages from the likes of McDonalds, Pepsi, Nike and Co. They are so imposing that I'm sure that they must be off-putting to the players – though the

---

[5] Mickel Sylvestre's body double was a white guy! As was Claude Makelalee's stunt double who had to be blacked up like a minstrel. Are there no black stunt men in Britain?

players will not complain, because the revenue from flashing hoardings goes to fund their high wages.

Other forms of entertainment are not violated in this way by overbearing advertising. When we go to the cinema to watch a movie, we get shown adverts before the trailers. Most of us accept this as being an important form of revenue for the cinemas. But imagine being in the cinema and having to put up with flashing advertising hoardings below the big screen – during the movie. It would no doubt affect a person's enjoyment of the film. On this occasion, the movie goer would not put up with an excuse such as 'But it brings in more revenue for the Odeon'.

It would seem that as football fans we have to put up with just about anything in the name of more money coming into the game. This style of advertising is aimed at the TV viewer (there are no flashing hoardings on the same side of the stadium as the main TV camera). The money-men of football were concerned that the game went a whole forty-five minutes without a commercial break, which is the same reason that football has never made it big in the USA. For football to break America it must have a credible TV deal, and US channels don't usually go more than five minutes without a commercial break, let alone forty-five minutes (when I was in America I saw a billboard advert for a TV station that boasted 'NO AD BREAK FOR TEN MINUTES – NO KIDDING!'). They've finally found a way to flash images into our heads throughout the whole ninety minutes and we're paying for the privilege. It's hard to believe that in the late 1970s and early 1980s, BBC sport had a conflict with the Football League about showing live football on TV because, for the first time, there were sponsors on the team shirt. The BBC were worried about breaching their own rules because they are not allowed to advertise any outside product. At the time they had no choice but to accept the change in football. Yet now they broadcast matches that feature flashing adverts for McDonalds and co and it goes completely unquestioned. Also, every time a player gets interviewed they make sure the player is standing in front of a plaque that displays a list of sponsors, and this is just BBC programming. Gone are the days of players being interviewed in front of a rack of boots!

Barcelona and Real Madrid were both famous for rejecting the idea of having sponsors on their team shirts. The reason for this was that they felt no advertiser was worthy of having their name displayed on their proud kits. Real Madrid gave into shirt sponsorship at the start of the millennium with Siemens mobile being the advertiser with enough money to tempt them away from their pride. In 2006 Barcelona had their first ever shirt sponsor as they agreed to be sponsored by the UN's children's charity UNICEF, in a five-year deal that did not involve money.

That in itself is an incredible gesture, as the club is prepared to lose tens of millions of pounds in favour of promoting a charity. Had Barcelona been sponsored by a commercial brand then it quite possibly would have been the biggest sponsorship deal in football history. Barcelona President Joan Laporta said of the deal "It's an initiative with soul. It means winning the Champions League on a social level. It shows the world that our club is more than just a club." The fans of Barcelona have always been very strongly principled and would not have tolerated a shirt sponsor from any other outside interest. A club able to resist outside commercialism, and yet one that is also so successful is an example to its rivals all over the world. Since the UNICEF deal, the only big club in Europe without a shirt sponsor is fellow La Liga club Athletico Bilbao in the Basque region of Spain. Athletico Bilbao, just like Barcelona is viewed as a kind of national team by the fans. Athletico Bilbao is seen as the unofficial national team of the Basqe region, in the way that Barcelona is seen as the unofficial national team of Catalonia. Of course national teams do not have shirt sponsors,[6] which is surprising for the commercial age we live in. The reason behind it being that no brand can possibly sponsor a whole country of millions of people. However, every year the game gets more obsessed with money and if football carries on the way it is right now, don't be surprised to see sponsors on the national team shirts in the coming years.

Commercialism in football will go way beyond the mark if advertisers try to get involved in team affairs. For example, if the clients were to try and have an influence on which players actually play for a team then it would be unacceptable. There have been plenty of allegations in recent years that Nike has had too strong an influence in the Brazilian national team squad selection. These allegations hit a height just before and after the 1998 World Cup. Before the finals it was alleged that Nike were picking the Brazilian team in favour of the players who they had contracts with. After the World Cup Final between Brazil and France there were allegations and conspiracy theories that Nike had insisted that Ronaldo play, even though he was physically and mentally not right for the final. Ronaldo was Nike's highest profile player and it was perceived that for him not to play in the final would have been a disaster for Nike. It does seem strange that Ronaldo played in this game. Even with his great reputation, no sane manager would have included him because he was quite clearly in such a bad way that night. But these are just allegations and conspiracy theories and no one has come up with ultimate proof to back this up.

But if a sponsor was ever found guilty of interfering with team affairs, then they should be banned from any further involvement with the game. It wouldn't surprise most people if this sort of interfering from sponsors does have a secret place in football, but never actually gets fully exposed. If it does go on then I wonder how quick FIFA would be to expose it, considering their

---

[6] The Republic of Ireland were once sponsored by car makers Opel.

own relationships with outside backers. The public's perception of their money-driven vision of football would no doubt be damaged by such a scandal (for an in-depth insight into just how corrupt FIFA can be, I recommend reading the book *FOUL! – THE SECRET WORLD OF FIFA: BRIBES VOTE RIGGING AND TICKET SCANDALS* by Andrew Jenkins.)

Whereas some fans won't accept a club sponsor on the shirt, others seem happy to let the very heart and soul of a club be bought out by outside interests. It's increasingly common in Europe now for stadiums to be named after advertisers instead of the club. Recently I've been a bit confused as to whether or not I follow Arsenal FC or Emirates Airlines or even both. The crowd at Arsenal are now even referred to by the media as the 'Emirates crowd' – not Arsenal supporters. Where I live in North London I have a view of Arsenal's new stadium in Ashburton Grove. In big red neon lights I can see those words **THE EMIRATES STADIUM.** The stadium is dominated by the signs of Emirates Airlines who have paid a lot of money for this honour, and what Arsenal got from this deal will eventually be worth £100 million over a period of years. This £100 million means that Emirates have rights to the name of the stadium for fifteen years and have the rights to sponsor the club shirt for eight years from 2006. It is a lot of money and for these reasons I've had other Arsenal fans try and persuade me that this a great deal for the club and that I should be pleased about it. They can try to persuade me all they want to but they won't get anywhere. I don't care how much money Emirates are prepared to pay because identity and pride do not have a price tag. The sum of £100 million also looks a lot less substantial when you consider that Arsenal make over £3 million for every home game. As a fan, I feel that this stadium branding is just another invasion of the traditions of the club I follow. The most important thing that a football club has is the stadium and the fans. The directors, players and advertisers will come and go, but the stadium and supporters will always be there. So to name a stadium after a mobile phone or a packet of crisps takes away a huge part of the identity of a club. When we lose our identity and sell our soul to commercialism, what's left to follow?"

The corporate branding of a club like Arsenal is supposed to be the compromise for success on the field. When the team wins trophies the fans are kept happy. However, in the inevitable seasons when the club does not achieve success, the fans are left with a club that represents a bland corporate image and a belittled identity. In other words we're left with nothing. I wonder if supporters of Coventry City feel a great deal of pride and identity from sitting in the NTL stand, or the Jewson stand, or the Coventry Evening News stand, or the Marconi stand, at their brand new Ricoh stadium?

There are other options to make money in this way that do not sacrifice the soul of a club. For example the sponsor can have their name on the stadium, but not in a way that is more dominant than the symbols and name of the club itself. For example how about – **THE ARSENAL STADIUM – IN ASSOCIATION WITH EMIRATES.** To me that would be acceptable because the stadium still carries the name of the club and the advertisers still get promotion. Real Madrid play in the Bernabeu stadium which is named after the Real Madrid legend Santiago Bernabeu. Above the stadium the word BERNABEU is lit up in big letters and you feel a great sense of history and tradition when you visit the ground. Certainly much more than if their stadium were named after British Airways or Burger King. If the Nou Camp at Barcelona were named after American Airlines then Clive Tyldesley would have to use an extra three syllables in most sentences when commentating. The greatest football venues in history have names that are part of football history – Old Trafford, San Siro, Anfield, Wembley, Nou Camp, Bernabeu, Maracana, Stade de France, Highbury, St James' Park, Olympic Stadium Munich, Villa Park,

White Hart Lane, Parc des Princes, Velladrome, Hamden Park, Celtic Park, Ibrox, etc. Do we really want to sacrifice this for the likes of NTL, Emirates, AOL, EDF Energy, T-Mobile, etc?

Some people say that football is a religion and, in a sense, it is. It's something you follow with devotion and not necessarily just a belief in a God or an afterlife. Without wanting to sound like Clive Tyldesley, the equivalent of a church or mosque for a football fan would have to be the stadium. Followers of other religions though would not be so happy to sell their soul to commercialism in the way that football does.

Churches these days are empty and short of money. But no matter how short of funds the church is, you will never walk down a street and pass 'THE ADIDAS HOUSE OF WORSHIP' or the 'WALKERS CRISPS CATHEDRAL'. Any mosque named after a brand would last about as long as a goat at a Black Sabbath concert. This is because the followers of these religions have a sense of devotion which is so strong that it can never be sold away to outside interests, and to have their place of worship named after a sponsor would belittle and cheapen their religion. Alex Ferguson once made the point that football fans should not have to pay admission to the grounds anymore because of the amount of money the game generates from television and advertising. Of course the irony is that the more money that has come into football from things like advertising, the higher cost supporters have had to pay at the turnstile. So as paying customers over the years we certainly haven't felt the benefits of advertising, as the more money the clubs get from outside ventures the greedier they get. The Emirates sponsorship of the Arsenal stadium coincided with the highest ticket prices the club had ever seen.

I hate this invasion of advertising that has consumed football, because as fans, when we follow our teams we're supposed to be taking a break from normal life. That normal life includes the commercial world that now seems to dominate the whole of society. In this day and age we're having advertising shoved down our throats day and night. There are even TV screens on buses now. No escape. I can't sit on a London double-decker bus and concentrate on the book I'm reading because some big mouth from a TV screen is telling me about the latest headache tablets. Night and day no matter where we seem to go we are being told that our lives are empty because we don't have a certain product.

I fear that the only cultural heritage that we will pass down to future generations will be a legacy of soulless commercialism. Something like football is supposed to be our escape from the 'reality' of this bland superficial world. Yet football is now the leader in this advertising age, and the more advertising consumes a club the less the fans feel the club belongs to them.

Chapter 6
Value for money...

"Our gate income will probably be the highest in the world. We will have 60,000 fans and higher priced tickets – and more premium [corporate] tickets than any other club in the UK."

Managing Director of Arsenal Keith Edelman – 2006.

When I read this quote in the *Evening Standard* I shook my head in disbelief, although it didn't tell me anything I didn't already know. Football's a rip-off, that's common knowledge. But what staggers me is that Keith Edelman had the audacity to happily admit this fact, in what even sounds like a boastful fashion, as if Arsenal fans should be pleased that their club will have the highest gate income in the world due to being charged more money for admission. Ten out of ten for honesty, but it sounds to me a quote in which Edelman has accidentally assumed that he was at an Arsenal board meeting and not in front of journalists who will then relate his intentions to the public.

How many businesses boast to their customers that they charge more than their rivals? Maybe this is a trend for the future of advertising which other industries should take a look at. I can picture a television advert from HMV. They have a new slogan for their marketing campaign. *'HMV top dog for music. And with higher priced CDs we're making more money than our rivals.'* I don't really think it would work would it? Maybe Edelman's words were in fact some sort of sly marketing ploy? When some season tickets are so expensive, owning one almost becomes a status symbol and an element of exclusiveness does work in attracting certain people to a product. In recent years, my team

Arsenal FC has felt like a members' club in which there are people unable to get in because their names are not on the list. This exclusiveness might very well appeal to a lot of the fans who are on the inside, but it's a dangerous game to play. A crowd that enjoys being exclusive and that likes to follow a successful brand, will not be the ones who stick by that brand when that club becomes a mid-table team or worse. These people like to be associated with success and when the team they support fails, it makes them feel like failures too. English football history proves that no club can ever avoid a period of mediocrity or worse. Clubs such as Manchester United and Spurs spent a season of the 1970s outside of the top division. More recently, who would have thought that Leeds United would have gone from a Champions League semi-final with Real Madrid to a league match with Crewe Alexandra in just two seasons?

In 2007 the question 'Do you think match tickets are good value for money?' was asked to supporters via the internet survey group the Football Fans Census. The result was conclusive to say the least.

Do you think match tickets are good value for money?

YES – 12%
NO – 88%

Any other business in which 88% of their customers thought that the company represented poor value for money would be in serious crisis. A year before this, the BBC programme *Football Focus* had asked the very same question and the result was exactly the same with 88% of fans thinking that football represented poor value for money. However, Brian Barwick the chairman of the FA, responded to the BBC survey by saying "I think we've got the balance just about right." Easy to say when you're head of the FA and don't have to pay for access to football stadiums.

The study from the Football Fan Census surveyed 2,000 supporters, and emphatically makes it clear that supporters feel that the industry is not giving them value for money, from the gate admission to even the refreshments and merchandise that are sold at prices well over the odds. Other questions and results from the survey are as follows:

Should Premiership clubs use increased TV revenues to cut ticket prices?

Yes – 96%
No – 4%

Have you got into debt through following your team?

Yes – 20%
No – 80%

Do you go to matches less often, or more often than you used to?

Less often – 56%
More often – 8%
The same – 36%

Would you go to more games if tickets were cheaper and more available?

Yes – 86%
No – 14%

Would you be happy to pay more for tickets if it meant your club could afford to sign a top-class player?

Yes – 22%
No – 78%

Have you been to watch a team lower in the league than your own because it is cheaper?

Yes – 26%
No but I would in the future – 16%
No – 58%

What do you consider to be the biggest 'rip-off' at matches?

Ticket prices – 49%
Merchandise/ replica kit prices – 21%
Food and drink prices – 28%
Non-applicable – 2%

What I found most incredible about this survey was that 20% admitted that they had gone into debt as a result of following their team. Getting yourself into debt through a mortgage or feeding and clothing your family is quite understandable – but football?

What doesn't fit with the results of these polls, is the contradiction that football continues to draw big crowds, a fact that the Premier League and the FA like to point out on a regular basis. However, what they should take into consideration is that the vast majority of the people that make up these crowds feel a great dissatisfaction about how they are being treated as paying customers. Football is a complacent industry which is always a weakness in any field, especially one where most of the customers are not happy with the product they are buying into. When 86% of fans say that they would attend more games if the tickets were cheaper, then that is a clear indication that our stadiums could be fuller. Crowd numbers have fallen slightly in recent years, making empty seats a commoner sight. At the start of the 2005-06 season, attendances were down at many Premiership clubs compared to the previous season. It was the first time top flight football had looked vulnerable for well over a decade. Most journalists and pundits put this attendance fall largely down to a lack of entertainment. At the start of the season there was a shortage of goals scored and lots of 0-0 draws. This was maybe one of the reasons for the drop in attendance, along with the uncompetitive and predictable nature of the Premiership. But football is not an industry where the majority of customers will buy into something on the basis of how much entertainment it provides. The simple truth is that the vast majority of football teams are not very entertaining.

I've got friends from Darlington who every year travel down to London for the Leyton Orient v Darlington fixture. I've accompanied them several times at the Leyton Orient away game, but I've yet to report any hint of entertainment. The football is poor, and the truth is that for a lot of fans the whole experience is more of a show of loyalty and passion than a pleasurable entertaining experience. It's precisely because football isn't out and out entertainment that the clubs get away with charging such outrageous prices. If people were out looking for entertainment would they really go to Grimsby Town on a regular basis? (Not having a pop at Grimsby Town, just an example). It's because football's a passion built on unconditional loyalty from its followers that clubs feel they can exploit them.

Other than a surprising campaign by *The Sun* in 2007, aimed at lowering ticket prices in football (surprising in that a newspaper owned by Rupert Murdoch made a stand against free-market greed), the media over the years have very rarely highlighted the issue, whether it be newspapers, TV or radio. I think this can only be because for a lot of them, it simply hasn't been an issue as they don't pay entry into football grounds. Every game they see is for free, therefore they haven't always put themselves in the shoes of ordinary fans, and have seemed blind to one of the biggest issues in football for years. It would seem that the media have now only just woken up to a problem that has been neglected for so long. Even though I have many disagreements with *The Sun* (as will become apparent in a later chapter about media scrutiny) you have to give credit where credit is due. Occasionally *The Sun* will take a stance against things like racism, animal cruelty and now, in this case, the rip-off culture in our national game. A cynical viewpoint will be that the owners of *The Sun* also own Sky Sports, who have the rights to broadcast league football in England. Falling crowds throughout the leagues are not good for television entertainment, and no one wants to watch a match on TV with empty seats all over the stadium. If that is the case then Murdoch's media are being smart in realising this potential problem, so that's not really a criticism.

The main argument from *The Sun's* campaign was that, with the amount of money that football generates from television and advertising, there is no justification other than greed for charging such outrageous prices. No newspaper can force a football club to lower ticket prices, only the fans can do that by a major boycott of football. However, being such an influential newspaper that is read by millions, the campaign from *The Sun*, if continued and sustained over a long period of time, is the best opportunity for supporters to wake up and realise that prices have to be reduced, not just by a tiny fraction – but dramatically. Certainly by more than the £8.35 that *The Sun* called for. When Bolton Wanderers responded to *The Sun's* campaign by announcing that they would be reducing season ticket prices by 10% for 2007-08, it was hailed by the newspaper as a great victory for the fans. Whereas any reduction in admission pricing should be welcomed, a 10% drop still maintains football as an overpriced attraction for its loyal followers. And the price reduction is only for season tickets not matchday prices. Even if they did include matchday prices, 10% off a £36 ticket (the price Bolton charge away fans for grade A games) is not a great victory for football fans at all. In fact the £3.60 'saved' wouldn't even buy a pie at Wembley Stadium! In the same week Chelsea boasted that they would be putting a freeze on ticket prices for the 2007-08 season – how commendable when the cheapest adult ticket for Chelsea home games was already £45. Arsenal also boasted that they would lower ticket prices for Carling Cup matches for 2007-08. Equally as commendable given that the Carling Cup is a second-rate competition in which Arsenal field a second string team.

The following is a list of ticket prices for Premiership clubs for the 2007-08 season. Most clubs have separate prices for what they call grade A, B and C games. For example a grade A game at Aston Villa would be their fixtures against Manchester United, Liverpool, Arsenal, Chelsea and Birmingham City. Lower grade games would be their fixtures against teams like Fulham and Reading. I've also included the prices that clubs charge away fans for grade A games:

Premiership ticket prices for 2007-2008

Arsenal

Grade A game – £46, £51, £55, £61, £66, £70, £94

Grade B game – £32, £35, £38, £42, £43, £49, £66

Kids – (A) £18 (B) £13

OAP – (A) £14 (B) £20

Charge for away fans – £46

Aston Villa

Grade A game – £29, £30, £32, £35

Grade B game – £27, £28, £30, £33

Kids – (A) £10, £19 (B) £9, £17, £19

OAP – (A) £20, £21 (B) £17, £18, £19

Charge for away fans – £30

Birmingham City

£25, £27, £30, £35

Kids and OAPs – £14, £15, £18

Charge for away fans – £35

Blackburn Rovers [7]

Grade A – £25, £30

Grade B – £15, £20, £25

---

[7] Along with Wigan Athletic the best value team in the division. Season tickets can be purchased for as little as £250 for both these clubs, and I would use Blackburn Rovers and Wigan Athletic as an example of fairness in admission pricing for their home supporters.

Kids – (A) £15, £20 (B) £7, £15

OAP – (A) £20, £25 (B) £10, £15

Charge for away fans – £30

Bolton Wanderers

Grade A+ – £31, £36, £39

Grade A – £28, £33, £36

Grade B – £24, £28, £32

Grade C – £21, £25, £29

Kids – (A+) £16, £21 (A) £14, £19 (B) £12, £16 (C) £10, £14

OAP – (A+) £24, £26, £28 (A) £22, £25 (B) £18, £20, £22 (C) £16, £17, £20

Charge for away fans – £36

Chelsea

£45, £48, £60.

Kids & OAPs – £15

Charge for away fans – £48

Derby County

Grade A – £33, £42, £44

Grade B – £31, £40, £42

Grade C – £29, £38, £40

Kids – (A) £17, £22, £23 (B) £16, £21, £22 (C) £10, £15, £16

OAPs – (A) £17,£22, £28 (B) £16, £21, £22 (C) £15, £20, £21

Charge for away fans – £42

Everton

£28, £31, £33, £34

Kids – £17, £19

OAP– £21, £23

Charge for away fans – £32

Fulham

Grade A+ – £40, £45

Grade A – £35, £40

Grade B – £30, £35

Grade C – £25, £30

Kids – (A+) £15 (A) £10, (B & C) £5,

OAP – (A+) 25, (A) £25, (B) £20 (D) £15

Charge for away fans – £40

Liverpool

Grade A – £32, £34

Grade B – £30, £32

Kids & OAP – (A) £25, (B) £24

Charge for away fans – £32

Manchester City

Grade A – £29, £35, £37

Grade B – £26, £31, £33

Kids and OAP – (A) £15, £20. (B) £13, £19

Charge for away fans – £30

Manchester United

£25, £30, £31, £33 £34, £38, £40, £42

Kids – £10

OAPs – £12.50, £15.50, £16.50, £17, £19, £20, £21

Charge for away fans – £35

Middlesbrough

£24, £32

Kids & OAPs – £15, £22

Charge for away fans – £32

Newcastle United

£32, £38, £47, £49, £53

Kids – £7, £17, £19, £20

OAP – £26, £32, £40, £44

Charge for away fans – £32

Portsmouth

£28, £29, £35, £37

Kids – £15, £22, £23

OAP – £20, £22, £26, £28

Charge for away fans – £35

Reading[8]

Grade A – £39, £41

Grade B – £36, £38

Grade C – £32, £34

Kids – (A) £20, £21 (B) £15, £16, (C) £10, £11

OAPs – (A) £31, £33 (B) £27, £29, (C) £22, £24

Charge for away fans – £39

Sunderland

Grade A – £30

Grade B – £25

Kids – (A) £15 (B) £9

OAPs – (A) £20 (B) £15

Charge for away fans – £30

Tottenham Hotspur

Grade A – £39, £41, £44, £50, £51, £61, £71

Grade B – £32, £34, £36, £40, £42, £48, £52

---

[8] All home tickets are £4 cheaper to club members.

Grade C – £27, £30, £32, £34, £35, £39, £42

Kids and OAPs (A) £19, £21, (B) £16, £18, (C) £14, £16

Charge for away fans – £39

West Ham United

Grade A – £43, £49, £55, £61

Grade B – £34, £43, £45, £49

Kids – (A) £21, £24, £27, 30 (B) £12, £15, £16, £17

OAP – (A) £23, £25.50, £28.50, £30.50 (B) £17.50, £19.50, £21.50, £22.50

Charge for away fans – £43

Wigan Athletic[9]

Grade A – £25

Grade B – £20

Grade C – £15

---

[9] For the 2007-08 season Wigan rewarded their supporters by lowering season ticket prices to what they were in the days when they were a League One side five years before.

Kids – (A) £10, (B) £8 (C) £8

OAPs – (A) £18, (B) £15, (C) £10

Charge for away fans – £25

What's important to remember is that the so-called cheapest seats only make up a small percentage of tickets that go on sale, and would usually be the ones in the most demand. The availability of tickets therefore on offer for most fans will be the ones that are higher priced. On top of the price of the ticket, fans are also charged a booking fee for tickets bought over the phone and internet. The English Premiership is the most expensive league in the world to follow. As a result the English league has become the richest league in the world. Can ordinary supporters feel any pride in the fact that the Premiership is the richest league in the world?

Because what this really means is that football fans overseas have more money in their pockets to spend on things other than football. The ticket pricing in European leagues is affordable to everyone. For example, a season ticket at PSV Eindhoven will only cost €200 euros (£170). A club that regularly wins the Dutch championship and usually competes in the later stages of the Champions League. PSV are just an example, and the price of €200 euros for a domestic season ticket is normal for most top clubs outside of England.

Football presents itself as being a family game, but the financial burden on families to follow football is high. Let's take a conventional family of 2.4 children who are on a reasonable household gross income of £35,000. If they are Chelsea fans then by using the most conservative and cheapest costs on season tickets (cheapest ones available), travel fares (all-zone London travelcards), food (£5 each) and match day programme (one programme per game) that family will spend roughly £2,200 on watching their team play home games each season. And that estimate doesn't include extra cost for cup games not covered by season tickets, club merchandise or anything else but the most affordable way for a family of four to follow their team. £2,200 for this family to watch Chelsea home games each season is roughly 10% of their yearly net income. If this is the burden for a family on a reasonable income of £35,000, then what about a family whose chief wage earner is on minimum wage? Well after tax, a person who works a forty hour week on minimum wage (£5.52 per hour) will take home £186 per week. If that person wanted to take their partner and two children to a Chelsea home game, then the cost involved would be:

Cheapest match tickets – (two adults to two juniors, booking fee not included) – **£120**

Travel – all-zone London travelcards. Two adult, two children – **£18**

Food and drink – £5 each – **£20**

Match day programme – one programme amongst four people – **£3**

Total cost – **£161**

This is a very conservative estimate. For example, this family might come from a county just outside London therefore the cost of travel would be higher than the cost of an all-zone London travelcard. Yet the total cost for this family for one football match will be 86% of the main breadwinner's weekly net income. I bumped into a friend in a pub before an Arsenal home game in the 2006-07 season. He had brought his wife and two young sons along to the game and had paid a face value price of £175 on tickets alone. This family came from Essex, so no doubt when including travel costs plus food and drink, the total price would easily top £200. As a former regular at Arsenal this man has had to limit the amount of times he takes his family to watch football each season because of the financial burden (this man earns a decent wage and runs his own business). So when they say that football's a 'family game', what they really mean is that football's a game for very wealthy families.

Had tickets cost this much in the late 1980s and early 1990s when I was a junior, then I would not have been able to attend anywhere near as many matches as I managed to during that period. It's ironic that in the days when I had virtually no money the one thing I could always afford to do was go to watch Arsenal play home games. I never throw away any tickets for events or shows that I have attended over the years. In a cupboard in my room I have stashed away hundreds of tickets ranging from football matches, concerts, theatre and other sporting events like cricket and boxing. Recently I was rummaging around this cupboard full of memories and came across some nice little reminders, including the ticket of the first football match I ever attended. This was Arsenal v Everton in the West Stand lower tier in the year 1986. At the time Everton were the league champions and they won the game 1-0. The price on the ticket stub read £4.50 (adult price, not junior). Twenty years later in 2005-06, in the last ever season at Highbury, the same ticket was priced at £39. It doesn't take a mathematical genius to work out that this ticket price rise does not mirror the growth in wages in that twenty year period. Even if the average person's wage has tripled in that time the equivalent price would be around the £13 mark not £39. In 1995 a seat in the Clock End at Arsenal was £10. By 2005 it was up to £35, a 250% increase in cost. How many people's wages went up 250% in that ten year period? As I looked at other ticket stubs from the same era it brought back to me just how little it used to cost to follow your football team.

In 2006, the *Daily Mirror* reported that the most expensive season ticket at Arsenal and indeed in the country is £100,000, which will buy you two seats over the space of three years as part of the exclusive Diamond Club membership. Executive boxes cost £65,000 per annum and can seat around ten people and are bought on three to five year leases. Other top tickets cost around £4,000 a season and have to be bought for a minimum of three seasons. I've been sent emails from Arsenal inviting me to pay £250 just to be on a waiting list for what they call the Club Level.

Disabled fans now have to pay a high price to attend matches in this day and age of greed in football. At Arsenal, disabled access to the games had always been for free at Highbury, but since the move to Ashburton Grove in 2006 the club decided to rake in the cash at every opportunity. In 2006-07 disabled fans were expected to pay between £442.50 and £1,250 a season, and that was only a half price figure as a 'concession' for the first season. So no doubt this price is likely to be way higher in the following seasons at Ashburton Grove. It had been claimed that the disabled fans had insisted that they must pay, but that seems very far-fetched. Some disabled fans may have held this opinion but not all of them. If this was true then surely the fairest option would have been to let payment be optional. Those disabled fans who want to pay can, those who struggle won't have to pay full price, and there are plenty of disabled fans who do struggle to meet these prices. For instance, disabled Arsenal fan Jamie Brown didn't seem to be insisting too loudly that he should pay hundreds for his season ticket. He told the *Daily Mirror* in 2006 that:

"Arsenal is my life. I don't know what I will do now. I can't work because I have spina bifida."

"All the fans in wheelchairs are in the same boat. The prices are beyond us."

"I've been going to Arsenal for seven years. The club says we should contribute and we're happy to do this. But the prices are way beyond our means. I've paid a deposit for the cheapest seat. But I can't afford it. And the view is rubbish."

Well what an ungrateful moaner this Mr Brown is. Doesn't he understand that it's his duty as much as anyone else's to sacrifice themselves financially so that some people within football can become even more prosperous than they already are? Okay, so Jamie Brown only gets £160 severe disability allowance a fortnight to live on. Big deal, where's my violin and box of tissues? What about the footballers who struggle to buy a Ferrari once every fortnight? I don't see anyone in wheelchairs crying for them. It will only take Mr Brown over five weeks of his entire yearly income to afford to watch his team play home games each season. And the state sponger has the audacity to complain about a little spina bifida as to why he can't work. Okay spina bifida can leave a person paralysed from the waist down, but he should thank the money men in football for contributing towards his disability allowance through taxes. He should also take into consideration that the more of his money that goes into Arsenal, the better back treatment the directors and shareholders can get through the top osteopaths.

Irony aside, this is the mountain's peak of greed within the game. It's quite disgusting that the poorest people in society like Jamie Brown are being cruelly shunned from top level football because of the financial strain of supporting a team. Suffering from spina bifida must be very difficult, but for someone like Jamie Brown following Arsenal has clearly been one of the saving graces of his life. Now this saving grace is something that comes with a high price to pay for the principle that people who are luckier in life can be super rich instead of just very rich. Chelsea charge disabled fans up to £850, Liverpool only give a 25% discount and every other Premiership club charges disabled fans for admission. The carers are usually allowed free admission but then again this is in line with standard practice elsewhere. What's needed here is more of a price range based on incomes and whether or not a disabled person is working or on benefits. For example I think that someone like Professor Steven Hawking could afford to pay full price for a match ticket.

However someone like Jamie Brown should not be expected to pay hundreds of pounds for supporting his team when the price is beyond his range. Theatres and cinemas don't let disabled people in for free either, but they do have discount prices and more importantly they are usually one-off experiences, unlike a football season ticket which is an invoice for hundreds of pounds.[10] Here's another quote from Keith Edelman on Arsenal's new corporate direction. "We have 9,000 premium seats. 2,000 at club level and 7,000 at box level. The revenue from those seats alone is nearly that of the 38,000 at Highbury." Okay, so 9,000 corporate seats at Arsenal's 60,000 stadium generate as much revenue on matchday as the 38,000 capacity at Highbury used to. The question to Keith Edelman therefore is: Why are you then charging such a high price for the other 51,000 fans? Why is Jamie Brown paying £442+ when at Highbury he only paid a tiny fraction of that cost? I suppose the easy answer to that question is – because they can. The likes of Arsenal can charge what they want because enough fans will cough up the money, and enough fans will also be on waiting lists and willing to pay the same prices.

What annoys me is that it would appear that a large percentage of football fans seem apathetic about the predicament of people like Jamie Brown and indeed their own predicament. Their attitude is the classic "I'm all right Jack" mentality. But it seems ironic that the same people who are happy to pay a high price for football are usually the same people who give themselves

---

[10] At some clubs season tickets cannot be paid in instalments. The full amount must be paid before the start of the season.

high blood pressure whenever the price of petrol rises. They appear happy enough to get ripped off following their football team yet moan about the cost of everything else on the planet. In September 2005 I was at Upton Park to watch Arsenal play West Ham United. At half-time there was a small event to celebrate the Olympics which had recently been awarded to London for 2012. This was greeted with vocal cynicism by many of the home and away fans, most notably because the cost of staging the Olympics would be very high. They were outraged that their council tax bill will go up by roughly £20 a year to pay for the cost of staging the London Olympics. Yet this £20 a year tax bill was still £17 less than the price of a match ticket for the fixture they were attending on this day. £37 for just ninety minutes which, by the way, ended in a 0-0 draw! The Olympics is the pinnacle of sport and will bring regeneration to a desolate part of London. It will provide better transport for the London area and it will create jobs and leave Britain with a much better legacy for sport in terms of facilities. It will also boost tourism as London will get the chance to showcase itself as the greatest city in the world to millions of worldwide TV viewers. It's things like tourism that make London such a prosperous city. £20 a year extra council tax seems like pretty good value for money compared with £37 to go to Upton Park for a 0-0 draw.

Recently I had a debate with a Chelsea fan who claimed that football did represent very good value for money, and that if I didn't like paying top dollar to watch Arsenal then I should go and support Leyton Orient or Barnet. I think this lad is missing the point entirely. I'm an Arsenal fan and I follow my team whether we play good football or bad football. As luck would have it we play good football and have won many trophies. I'm allowed to be unhappy at the prices my club charges without being told that I don't appreciate good football. Of course I appreciate good football, who doesn't? This man's been conned into thinking that successful clubs charge their fans more money than teams lower down the league. In the Premiership there's very little difference in ticket prices between the teams who finish top and the teams who finish bottom. In 2005-06, Birmingham City who were relegated that season, were more expensive to watch than Manchester United. At Birmingham during that time the cheapest adult tickets were £40 for grade A games, whilst at Manchester United the cheapest tickets for all matches were £23. During this debate, my main point to the Chelsea fan was that it is only in English football that fans are so heavily overcharged. He seemed surprised when I told him that a match ticket for top clubs in Europe could be purchased for as little as €10 euros. His comeback was that everything in England is overpriced. Not completely true, but there is a fair point in his reply. But surely then that's even more reason for football to be affordable now? When trying to pay the mortgage, the council tax, the bills, the car insurance, travel fares, the weekly food shop and everything else, do you really need to be hit with an £800 invoice from your club to pay for a one-year season ticket? The culture of professional football was not built on this principle. Football was an attraction that was accessible to people of all incomes.

If people like this particular Chelsea fan think that everything in England is a con then maybe it's because people like him say that "Oh well it's what you've got to pay" (which he did indeed say) when faced with a blatant rip-off. Football fans in other countries would unleash fury if they were asked to pay the same prices we do for football tickets. Hypothetically, if ticket prices were too expensive in Italy the Italian fans would probably use two tactics.

1. Refuse to pay and protest by staying away.
2. Burn the club down!

Result: ticket prices in Italy come down. Problem solved. Not absolutely everything in England is a con if you make the effort to find value for money. And that value for money includes other forms of entertainment. I can go to my local cinema for £3.70, sit in a comfortable environment and watch a film of my choice. I know a good quality London West End cinema that offers admission from £1 to £4. I could walk into any major London museum such as the Natural History Museum or British Museum for free. Or I could go to the world famous Shakespeare Globe theatre and watch a live performance for just £5 on a warm summer evening. I'd do it regularly if I understood a word of what Shakespeare was on about! (They have standing at the Globe – no Taylor report in place yet!). A top range ticket to watch the proms at the Royal Albert Hall can be purchased for as little as £12.50. Lower priced tickets start from £5. So-called middle class/upper class entertainment such as theatre and opera are now far cheaper than the so-called working class game of football. Tickets at the 'elite' Royal Opera House range from £6 to £140. Top drawer London West End theatres offer a cheaper night out than the London football clubs do on a cold wet Tuesday in January. At the time of writing one of the hottest tickets for West End theatre is the show *AVENUE Q* which is on at the Noel Coward Theatre in Covent Garden. These are the ticket prices for this show at the height of its popularity:

£10, £20, £25, £32, £37, £45, £49

The lowest priced tickets for West End theatre averages at just £10. But if you don't think that this is very good value for a night out in London, then you could always try the nearest football club to the West End which is Millwall FC. These are the adult admission prices for Millwall who, at the time of writing are two divisions below the Premiership:

£20, £25, £27,

AVENUE Q at Covent Garden, or Millwall v Yeovil Town? It's entirely up to you. I follow Millwall on the side and enjoy going down to the Den to watch a game. But I've also seen *AVENUE Q*, and people walk out of these kind of shows smiling and looking happier than many football fans do after spending over £30 to watch a 0-0 draw in the cold outdoors. Football can't claim to deliver the same customer satisfaction and that's where the problem lies when they charge such high prices in the name of entertainment. If you paid money to watch a West End show but felt the whole performance was poor, then the last thing you're going to do is pay money to watch the same show a week later. But this is the crazy way in which football operates. Unlike other forms of entertainment football doesn't have to satisfy its customers in order to maintain a healthy business.

Because of the increase in ticket pricing, football grounds have become predominantly middle class and exclusive to those who can afford it. Before every Arsenal, Tottenham or Chelsea home game, there are legions of Mercedes, BMWs and 4x4s making their way to the ground which is something that never used to be seen before football became fashionable. The problem lies not in the fact that these people like football and want to go to watch it. The problem is that the new breed has completely taken over and pushed out so many others.

My argument is not that the middle classes or high earners shouldn't feel at home at football grounds. I'm not against any class of person going to football, but that's the whole point. Football can only be the people's game if it's accessible to all the people. Today, football is accessible to either people with lots of money, or to people with little money but who dedicate all they have to supporting their club. So many of us don't fit into either of those two categories and so are unsure as to where we fit in with the modern game. We're paying more for football now, but overall is the sport giving us more satisfaction and fulfilment? Is football really better now than it has been in the years gone by? The wealth that has been generated by the paying customer has not really made football as a whole any more enjoyable. This was quite clearly highlighted by the 2006 World Cup which lacked great games and memorable moments in comparison to World Cups of years gone by. So then where's our value for money? If I had a Ford Fiesta but wanted a better car, I might buy a Jaguar: more value for money. If I wanted a step up from that, then I would then buy a Ferrari. The more money I spend, the better product I should be getting. In football I'm paying more money, but I'm not getting any more enjoyment out of the game than I was ten, fifteen, twenty years ago.

Of course football fans aren't the only ones who pay a high price in return for an environment where they are treated with contempt. For instance night clubbers, on a regular basis, before standing outside in a queue for an hour will:

1. Pay good money to get dirty looks from bouncers.
2. Get squashed like sardines in an overcrowded environment.
3. Queue at the bar for twenty minutes in order to buy an overpriced drink.
4. Listen to a bland choice of music they don't really like.
5. Give up on conversation because the music's too loud.
6. Claim they had a 'mad night' before taking out their frustrations in a drunken brawl later on in the evening.

But if a nightclub offers this kind of hospitality, anyone with a brain should easily come to the conclusion that they should never step foot into that particular establishment ever again. With football fans it's more complex than that. The brain doesn't always get to make the decisions as the heart gets in the way. It's tough to abandon something that has been part of your life from an early age. If you've followed a football club all your life then the football club becomes part of your identity. How easy can it be to temporarily or permanently abandon a part of your own identity? Scores of football fans would love to stage a form of protest by not buying match tickets. But many fans worry that if they do this, plenty of other fans will just take their place, and when this happens they've lost access to the club they support and will no longer have a way of even buying tickets. This is a tough decision for any fan to make and is the main reason why the football clubs get away with treating fans so poorly. In the last few years I've let both my brain and my heart make the decision as to whether or not it's worth going to matches on a regular basis.

If offered a season ticket by Arsenal (cheapest one £895) would I accept it? Absolutely not. The brain tells me that I'm sick and tired of paying well over the odds for something just so that people who are already rich can be even richer. The heart is now telling me that I don't feel strongly enough towards the principles of the modern game to continue to be a part of it anymore. I may be a football fanatic who still loves the game – but I'm not a mug. I will not pay a fortune to watch diving from overpaid players, to sit amongst boring fans, and to be ordered about by people in orange bibs. In two words: screw 'em!

Chapter 7
Football in the future...

I had this vision of the year 2028...

I'm in a pub called the Moon Under Water watching football on the big screen. This pub used to be known as The Freemason's Arms before it was taken over by a major chain. The Government recently passed laws giving tax breaks to the major chains for the more independent shops and pubs they take over. This was recommended by the Monopoly Commission which is headed by the wheelchair-bound old campaigner Rupert Murdoch. On the big screen, the commentary lets me know that the first five minutes of the first quarter "has been brought to you courtesy of the Carphone Warehouse".

In the stadium itself, the stewards and CCTV cameras are monitoring the crowd for instances of thought crime. One spectator slyly hands a note to the person in the seat next to him. The note reads - *I'm not happy with the five in midfield. We need more support for the front man*. This message is picked up by CCTV cameras and the two fans are dragged out the stadium and banned from the ground for life. Of course the term 'football fan' has finally been replaced by the now popular and more suitable phrase 'football consumer.' Another consumer is being thrown out of the ground for wearing club colours that were not purchased from official outlets. Other consumers have been ejected for causing offences ranging from bringing their own food into the ground, to standing up and cheering when a goal is scored for more than the regulated five seconds.

At half-time, a big screen TV in the stadium displays all the other results from the Nestlé English Super League.

NIKE TOWN FC	**1-0**	REEBOK WANDERERS
STARBUCKS UNITED	**3-3**	EMIRATES ARSENAL
MOSS SIDE MCDONALD	**1-1**	CHELSEA BOOTS
ADIDAS ACADEMICALS	**2- 2**	PUMA ATHLETIC
NEWCASTLE BROWN ALE	**0-0**	THOMPSON HOTSPUR
LEICESTER & ALLIANCE	**3-2**	NORWICH UNION

The consumers all leave the stadium at the end of the game. Some are in their best tuxedos and have official club scarves round their necks and baseball caps with the club's sponsor displayed on it. The good news is that wearing these baseball caps will soon be compulsory. They only cost €100 euros and the club receives money from the sponsor for every cap purchased. Some consumers are a little unsure about this marketing scheme but they understand that anything that brings money to the club is ultimately good for them also. On the way home, a group of consumers have a discussion on how the game could have done with a third act. One consumer insists that a third act might have been too much for the performers.

Meanwhile on the other side of the culture spectrum, our nation's opera houses have been generating a lot of concern and are gaining publicity for all the wrong reasons. A news crew catches footage of a group of Puccini fans who are having a tear up with a mob of Wagner supporters outside the Royal Opera House in London's Covent Garden. The Puccini fans get the better of things early on, but the Wagner fans have stamina and end up having the rival mob on their toes. BBC news reporter Hayden Prutt is quickly on the scene and asks these opera fans why it is they choose to behave the way they do. "It's what you live for every weekend, going to the opera, letting all that tension out." answers one gentleman with a broad Yorkshire accent. "Opera's about passion. Proper working man's entertainment. It's our buzz".

Hayden Prutt then interviews a smartly dressed lady who is sitting outside a coffee shop in Covent Garden. She represents the traditional opera fan from yesteryear. She wears a plush mink coat and has a well spoken accent. She still attends the opera despite having grown disillusioned with the route that it has taken in recent years, and she hopes one day that opera will return to its true roots. Hayden Prutt asks her "Can you remember a time when not all opera fans were poorly educated working class scum?"

She shakes her head in dismay. "In the old days opera fans could sit together. There was no need for segregation. Why can't these people follow badger baiting instead?" she moans before ducking for cover to avoid a Wagner fan being thrown through the coffee shop window. Hayden Prutt looks down on the Wagner hooligan who is lying on the floor covered in glass. He points to the man then looks into the camera and grins smugly. "However, scum like this can't claim to be real opera fans. They're just here for the fight. The real fans are still inside the auditorium watching the drama unfold."

Inside the Royal Opera house, the crowd are getting restless and irritable with what's been a lacklustre and poor performance of *Madam Butterfly*. One fan rises from his royal box and shouts out 'SHIT, THIS IS FUCKING SHIT.' Another upset fan in the lower circle calls out to the performers to 'SHOW SOME PRIDE.' The tension in the crowd rises even more with the poorly acted unconvincing suicide of Butterfly herself. This causes fights to break out in the stalls and even in the royal boxes, where some fans piss in wine glasses and throw the contents down on the people below. The Royal Opera house does not yet have steel fences between the crowd and the stage and it's not long before a stage invasion occurs and the performance is abandoned. Outside however, some fans have already left early in order to beat the traffic. Hayden Prutt is outside with them and gathers their thoughts on the night's entertainment

"They're not fit to wear the costumes," grumbled a Geordie who is then pushed out the way by a Scouser who whinges "I've been watching *Madam Butterfly* for fifteen years and that's the worst performance I've ever seen. Should dock 'em all a week's wages. They're a disgrace".

"Will you be coming back next week to see the show?" asks Prutt. "I've been coming every week since the Puccini season started," replies the Geordie. "Hopefully things will improve, but so far I've watched the same crap show and the same crap actors for fucking weeks now and I'm sick of it".

In the same week the BBC's controller Rupert Murdoch sends Hayden Prutt on a mission to Italy. He is there to follow English opera fans who have travelled to Rome to watch the English National Opera perform a version of *Tosca* – in English! This is when modern day opera culture is at its most damaging to the reputation of England, as bare-chested groups of English opera fans parade the streets of Rome and sing classics such as *Nessun Dorma*. They drink beer and perform poorly acted death scenes in full view of the public. Even though England hasn't produced a world class opera tour for many years, these fans still believe that one day England will be top of the world. Throughout the piazzas of Rome, St George Cross flags are tied to buildings and statues. One flag reads – 'Gilbert and Sullivan – Salford division'. As always with English opera tours, the shameful scenes overshadow the stage drama and there are calls for England to be banned from singing in Europe for at least five years. Shortly after the Italy trip Hayden Prutt gets to appear as a guest on the long running political show *Question Time*. The question of opera violence comes up, along with other topics such as whether or not politics has been dumbed down in recent years. Host Jade Goody chairs, to the best of her ability, in the bumbling but lovable way that makes her the nation's sweetheart. In this particular episode of *Question Time* she only let slip with the word 'fuck' on just three occasions, and only smoked two cigarettes. After the show the one subject that sticks with Hayden Prutt is the question of whether or not football has become too elitist. He doesn't feel as well informed on the subject as he'd like, so days later Prutt takes a camera crew to Soho Square to report on whether or not the sport needs to reach out to new fans in order to survive. He goes to visit the headquarters of the 'Football Consumers Association' who are now run by the Premier League. He gets an interview with the chairman, Lord Cornelius Dunseith. Hayden kicks off the interview with the most fundamental question in football.

Prutt – Cornelius. Is it fair to say that football is too elitist?

Dunseith –You see Hayden old boy, what we need to understand is that football has a certain etiquette that needs to be respected. You cannot have people coming to the football who behave in a way unfitting to the culture of the brand we offer.

Prutt – Behaviour such as?

Dunseith – Talking too loudly. Standing up during a performance. I can tell you stories about some of the people we've had at football which you just wouldn't believe. Have you heard the tale about the person who one day shouted out to the players?

Prutt – No.

Dunseith – It was one of those embarrassing moments when you just wanted to curl up and die. He did, horribly. But all credit to the players that day as they dealt with it very professionally and continued with the game.

Prutt – But ordinary people feel that they don't belong at the football. That somehow this is a sport for the elite only and for people with money.

Dunseith – There are no signs up banning the working classes from coming to football matches. They can come to the football if they want to.

Prutt – How much would a ticket cost them?

Dunseith – Tickets for the upper circle at most grounds start at around a grand a game. But the good news is that the clubs have agreed a freeze on ticket pricing for the next year.

Prutt – That's very commendable.

Dunseith – Yes. And if a person is on a low income but has savings, then there's no reason why at one time in their life, they couldn't just splash out on a day at the football.

Prutt – Their savings?

Dunseith – They might not live to see those savings anyway because the life expectancy of the lower classes is… er… well, lower.

Prutt – But their savings?

Dunseith – Well you can't take it with you when you pop off, and we're always willing to issue a ticket against the value of your property. It's only money Prutt. It's not everything.

Prutt – So you'd welcome these people at football stadiums?

Dunseith – Bums on seats dear boy, bums on seats. And if your bum's not on a seat during the game then your bum will be on the back seat of a police car. Ha ha, get it?

Prutt – That's very good. One from the 'Clive Tyldesley Easy-To-Make-Up Puns, Volume 6' I believe.

Dunseith – The very one. A genius of the day, a bloody genius. Some say Lord Byron. Some say William Shakespeare. Some might even say William Blake. I say Clive Tyldesley.

Prutt – Sir Clive Tyldesley.

Dunseith – Of course. Dear Clive how he'll be missed. You know that he had his ashes spread on the turf at the Nou Camp in Barcelona. Said that when he was gone he'll want people to come and visit him there just so they'll never forget that balmy night in that same stadium, when Manchester United came back against all odds, and when David Beckham and Ryan Giggs...

Prutt – We're going off the point a bit.

Dunseith – Yes. Anyway this is compete nonsense. At football grounds there are plenty of people from very poor backgrounds who attend every game of the season.

Prutt – Really? Do you have a special deal then for low earners?

Dunseith – Yes that's the one. The special deal – or the new deal – or something like that. The government were even kind enough to scrap the minimum wage law just so we'd be willing to offer these people employment and give them hope.

Prutt – So these people you refer to are actually hot dog sellers?

Dunseith – Don't be a fool Prutt. Hot dogs are banned from stadiums, health and safety. Could be used as a missile, take no chances. No, these people sell match-day programmes, ice cream tubs and binoculars.

Prutt – You just mentioned health and safety. You seem very concerned about unruly behaviour from the consumers you represent. What are your methods in clamping down on the trouble-makers?

Dunseith – We never have any trouble at our football grounds. In fact we haven't had one major incident for anything more than the usual bit of over exuberant thought crime, or not wearing official club merchandise.

Prutt – Why is this?

Dunseith – Zero tolerance. We're not prepared to put up with crime at our football stadiums. We have a highly advanced way of predicting crime and stopping the criminals before they have time to fight, swear, vandalise or pillage.

Prutt – Explain.

Dunseith – One of the best indicators of disorder is social class. The newspaper we read is a good indication of our social class. For example, scum read *The Mirror*. Therefore, we run spot checks on the consumers, and if they are found to be reading the wrong sort of newspaper, there is a fair chance they are hooligans. So we chuck the buggers out.

Prutt – And does this system work?

Dunseith – Well, you just have to look at the statistics. Although, due to our zero tolerance policy, the crowd trouble ratio is very high, most of the consumers haven't actually done anything, so in fact actual trouble inside football grounds is very low

Prutt – So football stadiums are a safe place to be?

Dunseith – Yes dear boy. If you're a law abiding football consumer, your chances of getting caught up in disorder are very low. Because it's far more likely you'll be ejected from the ground first.

Prutt – I'm sure that all consumers will drink to that…

Dunseith – As long as those drinks are purchased from the club bar though Hayden. Look, clubs are not afraid to use tough methods in dealing with scum at our stadiums. Take for example Nike Town FC. Last year they never had to make one arrest, nor did they not have one unruly incident.

Prutt – Impressive. How did they achieve this?

Dunseith – They, along with the police, made it a criminal offence to watch Nike Town FC play. So they played out the whole season to an empty stadium. The owners of the club were not prepared to let a minority of idiots ruin the enjoyment for the decent fans of Nike Town.

Prutt – But with an empty stadium didn't that cost them financially?

Dunseith – No Prutt, because you do these things after the season tickets have been renewed and paid for. And not only that, it leaves so much more space to fill the rest of the ground with flashing advertising banners and billboards. Genius, bloody genius. They deserved that Deloitte Money League Championship last season.

Prutt – And the consumers were happy with this?

Dunseith – It brought more revenue to the club didn't it?

Prutt – I assume so.

Dunseith – Well then, everyone's happy.

Prutt – Lord Dunseith, thank you very much.

Dunseith – You're welcome.

Chapter 8
The people's game...

"I would love to have an investigation to find out who invented football. We will never have to build him a statue or monument. He will always be part of history along with the greatest geniuses that ever existed. Those who invented penicillin, the telephone, television and gravity are the greatest geniuses of all time. But whoever invented football should be worshipped as a God."

Hugo Sanchez – Real Madrid and Mexico legend.

I've heard many people insist that the English have no recognisable culture other than morris dancing, royalty and cream teas. Many people perceive culture as being something foreign, exotic and colourful which it no doubt is. But culture is also something that our country exported to the rest of the world. My dad works in a secondary school in Hackney. The children were taken on a school trip to the city of Krakow, a university town in Poland. On return my dad asked a student how they enjoyed Poland and the student replied "It was all right, but it had no culture." My dad questioned this judgment and then came to understand that what this student meant by saying that Poland had "no culture" was that Poland had no black and Asian people. So in England some children are growing up believing that culture only applies to people from certain ethnic backgrounds. Cultural food for instance has come specifically to mean food from Asia, Africa or the Caribbean, so by this standard the French and Italians have no culture. Adults can take the blame for this as there are many in this country who are ignorant of how diverse culture really is. Maybe it's time to educate them. Culture classes perhaps:

Student – Sir, is sport culture?

Teacher – Yes sport is culture.

Student – What's the most popular sport in the world?

Teacher – Football.

Student – Who invented football?

Teacher – The English. Though the Scots also had a part to play as they pioneered the passing game.

Student – Oh! Is music culture?

Teacher – Yes music is culture.

Student – Name me some of the biggest bands of all time?

Teacher – The Beatles, The Rolling Stones, Pink Floyd, Led Zeppelin, The Police, Queen, The Who, Sex Pistols, The Clash, Black Sabbath, Bee Gees, Genesis… …I could go on.

Student – Where do they come from?

Teacher – All from England.

Student – Does writing count as culture?

Teacher – Yes literacy is culture…

Student – Who's the most famous writer of all time?

Teacher – It has to be William Shakespeare.

Student – Where's he from? [etc.]

As Brits we should know about the dark side of our history and the number of wrongs caused in certain parts of the world. But on the other hand, our country's gifts to the world in culture through sport, music, literature, engineering and science is also unrivalled and undervalued. If there is a discussion about Britishness or what it means to be British, clichés such as tolerance, fairness, and politeness are brought up, yet nobody ever mentions creativity, genius or ingenuity.

When Brazilians play beach football in Rio, it's something that has come about through the influence of English culture. When the Rolling Stones performed in front of a million fans on the Copacabana beach in Brazil, the people of that country were watching a combination of British and American culture. So it's fair to say that British or English culture through entertainment is a bit more diverse than just a group of men in funny trousers dancing around a flagpole.

In the last chapter we had a quick look into the future. Now let's go back in time. We're in a pub in London's Covent Garden. It's a pub called the Freemason's Arms. The date is the 26th October 1863.

Representatives of eleven football clubs have popped in for a quick pint and a chat about a spiffing idea they've all had about creating a new world phenomenon. The directors and executives of these eleven clubs start to get excited about an idea they've had of creating a unique brand – a business. Something with which they could exploit members of the general public for profit. A new social scene where they could sell lots of replica shirts of up-and-coming football giants like the Old Etonians and Royal Engineers. They had plans to play this new game in front of thousands of spectators who would spend lots of money on merchandise, pies and season tickets in well-decorated Victorian corporate boxes. They could even foresee a time when they could film the games and then sell the cinematic rights for billions of pounds to the local picture palaces, where men with slick moustaches would watch the games projected onto the big screens (look at the old film footage to prove that the game was ten times faster in the late 1800s!). These chaps in the Freemason's Arms were out to make a fortune.

Well actually hold on a second, that's not true, I'm lying. These men were sports enthusiasts who played a crucial role in one of England and Scotland's greatest gifts to world culture. They drew a clear line in the rules between Football and Rugby and the Football Association was founded. The rules later drawn up from the FA would form the modern game as we know it today. A small book containing just thirteen laws would by this day and age be responsible for 1.5 million football teams and 300,000 recognised clubs around the world. The Freemason's Arms still exists, but for some reason does nothing to advertise or boast about their claim to fame in world heritage. No plaque, no pictures, no anything. I get the feeling it's more of a rugby pub, but come on fellas, make an effort. It's an important part of history and something to be proud of.

Prior to the late nineteen hundreds, there had been lots of rowdy ball games played in England dating back to at least 1314, usually with the ball being an inflated pig's bladder – sometimes, according to legend, with the ball being a severed head! Even before that time, legend has it, that in the city of Chester, the Anglo-Saxons played football with the heads of defeated Danish invaders. According to historians, the ball games in the fourteenth century were a kick and rush free-for-all played around town centres - a tactic that the Wimbledon team of the 1980s and 1990s used with some degree of success. In 1314 Edward II banned these games with the threat of imprisonment for anyone who disobeyed the law. Edward III also banned football as it was stopping young men from practicing their archery, which at the time was vital for England in times of war. In later centuries in England and Scotland, whole towns would compete against each other in which the field of play would stretch from one town to the other. Some of these towns still carry on the tradition to this day.

There are some Italians who claim that football first started in Florence from a game by the name of Calcio, but that claim is a load of coglioni! Calcio bears more resemblance to football hooliganism than Association Football. It's legal thuggery in which bare-chested Italians in colourful trousers spend more time punching opponents and team mates than worrying about where the ball might be. And more importantly, Calcio is not a game played with the feet, unless you count the occasions when the players kick each other in the head. In fairness there are similarities to football, and Calcio was for the time revolutionary. It is arguably the platform of a style of team sport that resembles games like rugby, NFL, hockey and football. The ball is round, the pitch is rectangular and two teams (27 players on each side) compete against each other to get the ball to the opponents' end of the pitch. But claiming Calcio to be the original football is like the inventors of medieval music claiming the credit for inventing rock and roll. Football has a style of its own, different from Calcio in rules, tactics, method, skill and finesse. Calcio is still played in Florence to this day and is possibly the most violent barbaric team game in the world. It makes Aussie Rules, Ice hockey, IKEA openings and WWE all look like a non-contact game of tag.

The men in the Freemason's Arms in 1863 were from the upper classes. The pioneers and players of football were from the elitist public schools such as Eton and Harrow. In these early years the working classes would have had little or nothing to do with football. Sport owes a great deal to the people of these hierarchic public schools, but football could only expand and draw huge

160

crowds by becoming the people's game. It's interesting, that the elite of Britain created a sport that would arguably become the main representative of working class culture and lifestyle. The church played a big part in promoting football, as sport was seen as good for local communities.

Through the efforts of missionaries, football became popular in working class towns in the Midlands and Northern England. The teams in these towns and cities were formed in local pubs, factories, social clubs and churches. To use two examples: Manchester United was formed by railway workers in Manchester and Celtic FC was founded by the Catholic community in Glasgow.

In 1883 the balance of football changed forever when Blackburn Rovers won the FA Cup by beating Old Etonians in the final. The oldest cup competition in the world had started in 1872 and prior to Blackburn's win, the first twelve years of the competition had been dominated by the upper class amateur teams like Wanderers and Old Etonians. Blackburn Rovers were the first working class team to win a major football trophy. It was a landmark game as after that final in 1884, the public school amateur teams fell away while the teams from working class towns became the dominant forces of football. It's worth noting, that as soon as football became popular amongst the working classes, the upper classes dropped it like a bad habit and played rugby instead. The sport had become the people's game and would continue to be for decades to follow. All of the working class teams that created the first ever football league in 1888 are still famous names in English football and have league status.[11] It wasn't until one hundred years after the formation of the first ever football league, that the owners of football clubs in England deserted the very

---

[11] Everton, Bolton, Aston Villa, Blackburn Rovers, WBA, Wolves, Stoke, Notts County, Burnley, Preston North End, Derby and Accrington were the teams who formed the world's first ever football league.

people who built these institutions and made them the great names that now are marketed as brands and products.

So let's quickly go forward again to the modern day in search of the people's game. In the summer of 2005, football was put in the shade by what's been described as the greatest Ashes series of all time between England and Australia. At the beginning of the last day of the final test series, England were in a great position to retain the Ashes for the first time in seventeen years. All they had to do was stay in bat for the day or build up a lead so big that the Aussies wouldn't have enough time in the day to win the game. The day started off fairly well, however wickets soon started to fall. With four wickets already down, Freddy Flintoff was then caught by Shane Warne, and all of a sudden England had only 5 wickets in hand and a lead of only 126. After being in such a great position, it looked like England were going to fall short on the final day and fail to recapture the Ashes. At this point I felt devastated and turned off the television for the third time in about fifteen minutes. A couple of minutes later I turned the television back on and endured the tension which was almost too much to take. I soon realised that for the first time another sport had as much of an emotional hold over me as football. I'd always been a big cricket fan but the Ashes of 2005 were special and reinforced what a great game it is.

England won the series and a lot of people who had never watched cricket before jumped on to the Ashes bandwagon in similar fashion to the way people jumped on the football bandwagon in the 1990s. During the summer of 2005, people reacted positively to cricket for a very simple reason. As a sport it still felt traditional and authentic. It didn't feel corrupted or belittled by corporate branding, agents or overpaid players.

The English and Australian players all competed with great sportsmanship and integrity. The television coverage was very good and the commentators were light-hearted and showed a real love and knowledge of the game. At the time of this Ashes series, the perceived upper class game of cricket did almost feel like the people's game for these traditional reasons. The worry for cricket now is that it will go down the same overbearing commercial route as football. They've certainly made a very big mistake by selling the television rights of all England games to Sky Sports. The 2005 Ashes series would not have achieved the same popularity had it not been aired on terrestrial television. The Sky cricket deal is a short-term solution where the cricket authorities have put the popularity of the sport second to a better cash deal. This ultimately will cost the game of cricket many fans in the years to come.

After the Ashes in 2005, it was claimed that cricket had burst the football bubble. It hadn't, but what cricket had shown the nation in 2005 was an example of integrity and professional pride that football has lost in recent years, both on and off the field. The public want to believe in a sport that represents more than just bland commercialism and greed. They want something in which they feel part of rather than just being a voiceless spectator. During the summer of 2005 cricket was a sport that encapsulated a sense of old-fashioned romance. Those who lived near the Oval stadium got a view of the game from their flat windows and I'll always remember the TV pictures of people sitting on rooftops enjoying the cricket and the sunshine with a can of beer. It brought back memories of the way that football used to be when fans would sit on the stadium rooftops during a sell-out game, before the current culture of all-seater stadiums and an obsession with health and safety.

At the very heart of the people's game should be a sense of belonging. I recently asked a friend why it is he doesn't attend football matches any more. His answer was one that highlights the most important thing that football has lost in recent years. He replied "There's no sense of community any more. There's not many places I've ever felt like I fitted in, but I felt comfortable and

163

at home at football. Now that's gone. I look at football now and think, what's in it for me?" Football must offer something more than just simply being a sport. Most supporters follow teams who play mundane uninspiring football. The majority of fans will be disappointed in their team's performance at the end of the season. Therefore football supporters need to cling to a sense of pride in the club in order to stay loyal to their team. If that gets completely lost, then football won't survive, starting with the lower divisions. The football club is at times the biggest representation of the area and the community. There's only one team in all four English divisions that is not named after a local area and that's Arsenal who are named after a gun factory.

Every other professional football club in England is named after a district, town or city followed by a second name such as City, United, Athletic, Rovers etc. For this reason I've always found it hard to understand fans who support clubs hundreds of miles away from where they live. London for instance is bulging with Liverpool and Manchester United fans who've never been north of Luton let alone Anfield or Old Trafford. I'd even go as far as saying that Liverpool are the best supported team in London, especially amongst my age group who grew up in the seventies and 1980s. When Liverpool won the Champions League in 2005, the next day the team had an open top bus parade that took the players though the city of Liverpool. Thousands of Scousers came out onto the streets to celebrate as the bus drove past old terraced houses and tower blocks on the way to the city centre. Surely then Liverpool FC must mean far more to those people than it would to the Liverpool FC fans from Norwich who would have watched the open top bus parade on television?

A sense of belonging is built up from the people with whom you watch the games. It's important to feel affinity with the fans who fill the stadium. It's this rapport that keeps fans loyal to a club much more than the performance of the players. The all-seater stadiums have virtually destroyed this culture as friends find it hard either to buy tickets or, if they do have tickets, they can end up in separate parts of the stadium. Towards the end of the 2005-06 season that sense of community returned to a small group of us who found a way to get in to Highbury by unofficial means. Right in the corner of the old North Bank there were always enough spare seats held back which for some reason the club would never put on sale, so once inside the ground we always found a place to congregate. The club never gained money from me being there but I didn't give a damn about that. Most of the other lads who got in the ground unofficially would buy beers and food at half-time so the club still made money from us being there. An average of thirty of us would watch from this corner of the ground and get to see the final games that were played at Highbury. From that point on it didn't matter that the rest of the stadium was quiet and lacked atmosphere. All that mattered was that the thirty of us had our little section of the ground and supported the team in our own way. During some big games there would be nearer one hundred of us in that corner. The thirty or so of us who were regulars were not all close friends, or even friends at all. But we were familiar enough with one another to all have a good laugh and make some noise throughout the game, which was in contrast to the majority of the fans in the stadium.

One of the last games of that season was against Charlton Athletic on a sunny but cold afternoon in March. Too cold to sit down in silence that's for sure, and when it's nippy you need to warm yourself up. Our little section was vocal as ever but as usual the rest of the crowd looked unenthusiastic, even when Arsenal were 3-0 up. In fact it was so quiet, that from twenty rows up in the stands, we virtually had a conversation with Dennis Bergkamp who was warming up on the touchline. At one point in the second half, thirty of us turned to the rest of the North Bank and chanted "Shall we sing a song for you?" A song usually sung in irony that is directed at opposing fans. This was greeted with thousands of scornful looks back, but it felt fantastic. We'd managed to offend a stand of 10,000 people and in a non-aggressive humorous way. Only a tiny handful of people stood up and chanted back at us. I'd been waiting years to make my feelings known to the new breed of football consumer. When I finally did at the Charlton game in the final season at Highbury, I have to say that it felt good. Other chants directed at our own fans were "Can you hear the North Bank sing?" and "Are you Tottenham in disguise?" The North Bank were clearly offended but were either too apathetic or too spineless to direct a comeback at us. How can a stand of thousands let a small group of thirty people mock them and say nothing back in response? The Arsenal crowd of the 1980s and 1990s that I was part of would not have tolerated an insult such as "Are you Tottenham in disguise?" especially from fellow supporters.

Does the lack of community at football matches reflect what some people perceive as a lack community throughout Britain?

It would appear that a lot of people don't really know their neighbours any more, and have little or no contact with the people next door. My neighbours moved in two years ago and we haven't even got to the 'hello' stage yet, let alone gone so far as to actually have a conversation (so much then for the 'chattering classes'!).

So when neighbours can go through life without talking to one another, football fans can sit next to one another for a whole season and not speak a word. What happens when one person annoys a whole train carriage by playing music too loud on their mobile phone? Chances are that the whole carriage will tolerate it because they don't feel comfortable enough to stand up for themselves. They're unsure as to whether or not the rest of the carriage will back them up if they speak out. I know that I wasn't backed up by anyone when I told one mouthy teenager to "Turn that shit down" after he rudely refused my initial polite request to lower the volume of his mobile phone speakers. It seems that every time I get on a bus or train now, I have to ask a teenager to turn down the music on their mobile phone because nobody else will, even though people find this new trend highly irritating (for the record, I've found that if you ask politely, most people will turn down their music). So in today's Britain, a football stand of 10,000 people can let 30 people make fun of them and say absolutely nothing back in response because they don't know or trust the community they're amongst. If there is no community at football anymore then surely the game is dead even if it does make millions.

So what of the men who created the Football Association in the Freemason's Arms back in 1863? Could they have had any idea that what they were pioneering would spread across the globe to become the world game? Could they have imagined how much joy, drama, pain and ecstasy they would be responsible for? Would they have dreamed that an estimated billion people would tune in to the World Cup Final which is the ultimate pinnacle of the thirteen laws that they drew up? These were people who were fiercely opposed to the professional game and believed in sport being amateur – much like the attitude in rugby until it turned professional in recent years. In the early days of football many of the players came from great wealth so to not get paid for playing was not a big issue. When football was taken over by businessmen, and played predominantly by the working classes, the game had no choice but to become professional, and rightly so. But if these men were so opposed to the professional game then one can only imagine what they'd think of players earning over £100,000 in a week. I'm sure they would feel great pride at creating a game that took the world by storm. But they might also look down at the money-driven game as it stands today, and feel that what they created all those years ago has become somewhat lost.

Chapter 9
The game in the balance – part 2

Negatives continued

<u>Annual kit changes</u>

I'm surprised that there's enough polyester in this world to deal with the number of kit changes that go on every summer. It staggers me that any Newcastle United fan would need to buy a Newcastle shirt more than once every few years. It 'changes' every year, but for those of us not paying attention to minute detail, the Newcastle strip appears to be black and white stripes with black shorts every season.

This used to be something that Manchester United would be heavily criticised for but is now common for all clubs. When I was a kid, replica kit changes happened no more than every two years. Yet now, the home and away kits get changed every year without fail. This we are regularly told, is more of a problem for parents than those of us without children. It's been many years since I've bought a football replica shirt.

I don't have anyone putting pressure on me to buy the latest team kit, but the question is who does? People claim that children get teased by their friends if they wear an old football team kit instead of the most up-to-date one, and this is the common complaint as to why annual kit changes are a problem for many families. But is this a myth? I've worked in a junior school and I have to admit that I never saw an example of this sort of teasing that we're told goes on regularly. There were kids who would wear old football tops and in truth it always went totally unnoticed. Kids just love having the current team kit and that's understandable. They're just more likely to hassle their parents into getting them something that they really want, and then claim that other kids tease them as a very good manipulative excuse. This kind of teasing never happened in my old secondary school either. Kids would get ridiculed for wearing the 'wrong' trainers etc, but not for wearing an old football shirt. Children today are far more likely to be teased for not having a mobile phone than for having the 'wrong' football kit.

The con with annual kit changes is in the retail price, which is £40 on average just for a team shirt. £40 for something that should be for free – yes free! Football fans are now walking billboards. All over the country landlords get paid decent sums of money for allowing advertisers to put up commercial billboards on their properties. But football fans do it the other way round. We like to pay someone else so that we can advertise for them. The Manchester United kit is an advertisement for AIG and the fans are paying a lot of money for the privilege to advertise this product. This is not an exaggeration because on modern football kits the most prominent and domineering feature is the sponsor. But who can blame the advertisers or the football clubs for this? I don't, because unlike attendance at matches I don't believe that having the latest replica kit is an essential part of supporting your team. If supporters think that replica shirts are a con, then they shouldn't buy them and the price will soon come down.

<u>Shirt numbering</u>

Last time I counted there were eleven players to a team. Goalkeeper is number 1, your right back is 2, your left back 3, centre backs are 5 and 6, midfield starts at 4 and so on. But I suppose that was a little too simple and practical to keep, and more importantly not as profitable. Look at the previous negative for the answer as to why shirt numbering at football now goes even higher than the amount of years it's been since Spurs last won the title. After looking at each Premiership team's website, the highest squad number I could find was at Newcastle United, who had a player with the number 54 (currently nine years more than Spurs last title win). The method behind it is sneaky but very smart, because there's no actual need for squad numbering. The whole purpose of squad numbering is to encourage fans to spend more money by getting the player name and number printed on a newly bought team shirt.

Having the name of a club legend along with the team number printed on a team shirt is understandable. But it hardly makes sense to have the name of a current player on your back, who could leave the club the next day for a slightly better wage deal elsewhere. And speaking of those big wage deals…

Wage demands

When Roy Keane criticised the lack of atmosphere (and provision of prawn sandwiches!) at Old Trafford after a Champions League game against Dynamo Kiev in 2001, he should have taken a look at his pay cheque. When some players demand somewhere between £50,000 and £130,000 a week, then a large percentage of the money they ask for comes from the paying spectators through a massive rise in ticket pricing. This no doubt changes the type of fan that populates football grounds, and it would be fair to assume that most of the fans at a ground like Old Trafford are probably not hard-up kids from Salford who might actually bring the passion that some players demand. Thierry Henry also complained about the thousands of Arsenal fans who leave the Emirates Stadium early in order to beat the rush and get an easier ride home. There are plenty of loyal fans who have been priced out and who would stay till the end, but what's more important to the players – £100,000 a week, or better support? The fans that Roy Keane and Thierry Henry have criticised are the ones that footballers themselves are responsible for due to obscene wage demands that have gone beyond any logic and justification. I agree with what Roy Keane said about the lack of passion from the fans, but would Keane have compromised 1% (£500) of his wages for more passion from the stands at Old Trafford?

I'm not against high wages in football for those who deserve it. They're the masters of the most popular game on the planet, they provide entertainment and they carry the responsibilities and pressures of being in the public eye. Many players still come from poorer backgrounds and football gives them a better chance of gaining wealth than most professions.

Johan Cruyff once said "If a whole stadium is filled each week, and millions of fans are watching you on television, then we want to see some of the profit also." What these athletes do is far more than 'just kicking a ball about' and nobody can seriously argue that footballers don't deserve to be well paid for what they do. Especially when they generate such wealth for others. But when a victim of the 2005 London bombings who lost both legs and an internal organ, receives less compensation to live on for the rest of his life than some player's weekly salary, then just maybe the wages footballers now earn have gone beyond both common sense and value.[12] It's certainly a contrast with 1960 when Jimmy Hill successfully led a campaign to put an end to the maximum wage for footballers, which at the time was £20 a week.

"The maximum wage went because we had the public on our side. We got them to understand the unfairness of the situation where there was a limit, however talented that player might be,

---

[12] Danny Biddle lost both legs and an internal organ in the 2005 London terrorist attack. The Criminal Injuries Compensation Board awarded him only £118,000 to live on for the rest of his life.

compared to say a bank manager or a cricketer, that his salary was tied forever. It was public opinion that got rid of the maximum wage." – **Jimmy Hill**

The supportive public opinion that Jimmy Hill spoke of would today no doubt swing in the other direction. The general public look at the salaries which some footballers now earn in both disbelief and disgust. Especially in comparison to the wages of those who quite literally save lives in the jobs that they do.

Many people now believe that it's time to bring back in a cap on footballers' wages. The main stumbling block to a wage cap is that the European Union could step in and deem it illegal; because it is a restriction of earnings (the European Union is a fine example of how hard it is to apply both consistency and common sense). A restriction of earnings! Even when any wage cap in football would probably no less than £50,000 a week?

How about a wage cap of £12,000 a week? At least then we'd be spared from hearing the phase "That's more than I earn in a whole year" when talking about the money these guys earn. A person on minimum wage, who works full-time, will earn around £12,000 a year (before tax). A footballer who thinks that £12,000 a week is an insult would still be free to move on to another profession where they think they could earn a better wage. Or they could get a second job in a supermarket which they could fit in after training. With any luck that second job could earn them another £12,000 a year to live on. Let's be honest about this, most top flight players are not worth as much as £12,000 a week (£624,000 a year). It is a damn good wage and one that would still maintain footballers among the highest earners in society. Truly great players who believe they are worth more than £624,000 a year would be able to sleep easy, because they will earn far bigger sums of money through things like sponsorship, advertising and computer game royalties. It is by other means that top footballers earn most of their fortune anyway.

Wayne Rooney's annual earnings is reported to be around £8 million a year, but only £3 million of that comes through his weekly contract at Manchester United. The estimated £5 million Rooney earns through other means does not burden the paying spectator in admission prices. Players who think they're worth more than £12,000 a week, but who don't earn money through these other means are perhaps not worth as much as they think they are, because sponsors unlike football clubs don't pay high figures for those with no value. I don't like to play on a stereotype such as accusing footballers of being stupid, because they're not. Tactical awareness on a football field shows intelligence (and I bet that an IQ test taken by footballers wouldn't be that much different from the national average). On the other hand though, football is part of a culture in which someone like Graham Le Saux was deemed an 'intellectual' simply because of reading *The Guardian*. That's fucked up! What do they nickname a man who wears glasses – Steven Hawking? Any footballer caught doing a crossword would no doubt get the nickname Einstein. Put it this way: I don't think there are too many footballers out there who would make £12,000 a week as anthropologists or physicists.

As the European Union would be likely to put a block on a player wage cap then the only other answer to this problem is a limit imposed on the clubs as to how much of their yearly revenue they could spend on player wages. This would certainly put a stop to a club like Chelsea spending millions on player wages while making huge losses amounting to almost double their annual revenue. An argument against UEFA restricting player wages through any method would be that some of the best players in the world might move away from Europe to the United States, where they could potentially earn more money. Well if that were the case for some players then I simply say – let them go. The leagues of Europe would be better off without such mercenaries. If they were to choose to play in a Mickey Mouse league for the sake of a little bit more cash, then that would only prove their hearts were more concerned with greed than a great legacy within the sport. Let them waste their career in the MSL, because the truth is that a great legacy for a player can only be achieved in the big leagues of Europe and South America.

It's thought that some clubs in England spend between 60% and 70% of their annual turnover on player wages. The Premiership has the highest wage bill in world football at around one billion pounds per annum. Player agents argue that if you look at the revenue that football clubs generate then you'll find that player wages are justified. Correct, in relation to club revenue (except in the case of Chelsea) it's true that player wages are justified and they're getting their fair share. However it doesn't take a genius to work out that player salary demands have increased the revenue of the clubs. At the time of writing, the highest paid Premiership players are John Terry and Michael Ballack who are reported to be on £130,000 a week contracts at Chelsea. Despite this king's ransom, Ballack still had the audacity to moan about the cost of house prices in London, and to say that he was better off renting because buying was too expensive! Well I blame the Government for ignoring Ballack's problem. They should be looking into creating more affordable housing for first time buyers who earn £130,000 a week.

This gulf in wages between 'normal' people and footballers makes fans feel distant from the players. Players can be multi-million pound superstars before they've even achieved success in their careers. It makes it hard for fans to feel sympathy towards a player who is going through a difficult moment in his career. Why should fans feel sorry for a person who earns tens of thousands a week for not doing his job properly? Empathy is also lacking in regard to footballers earning time off from work. Again this is down to the high wages that have created a distance between players and supporters. Footballers do not get enough rest between the end of one season and the beginning of the next. Just one week after the 2006 World Cup Final, Premiership teams were playing friendly matches in preparation for the new season. During that time, Thierry Henry claimed that he only had twelve days off in one year. No matter how much money a person is paid, the human body still has its limitations. All professional athletes need time to refresh their bodies after a long tough season, and players should come back to pre-season training gagging for football, not feeling like they haven't had a holiday. But now the attitude from many fans and journalists will be that if players are so highly paid then they should simply get on with the job instead of complaining. When fans believe that they can no longer feel affinity and sympathy towards players, then it takes away the humanity from the game and makes football devoid of good spirit.

Even the gulf in wages between players at the same club must surely cause tension and problems. A player who performs well on £20,000 a week has every right to feel aggrieved when his team-mate who earns £80,000 a week is out of form and on the substitute bench. In the MSL, David Beckham earns more money in one day at LA Galaxy than most of his team-mates will earn in a whole year. That is potentially very unhealthy for team unity, and his reported £500,000 a week could be viewed with resentment from many of his team-mates if he doesn't perform to a decent standard every single week. But then how do you perform to a £500,000 a week standard? Sell more replica shirts is the answer, though that would be no consolation to the rest of the LA Galaxy team who have bills to pay.

One argument for footballers being so highly paid is that football is a short-lived career. Retirement for most players will come in their mid-thirties. So let's compare a footballer's predicament to athletes of another high-profile sport (or in this case, sports entertainment). Wrestlers contracted to the WWE (formally known as WWF) have a massive global superstar profile and are watched by millions of people around the world each week. WWE wrestling is different to other sports because the final outcome of a match is pre-arranged. In fact the regular WWE weekly TV show *RAW* is more like a soap opera with writers and rehearsals. But the competitors themselves are still athletes with pressures to be successful and entertaining in their profession. On average they're asked to compete a minimum of four nights a week in non-televised house shows (footballers moan at two games a week). Their dedication to their sport inevitably leaves them with lifelong injuries. There's nothing fake about being slammed though a table or being smashed round the skull with a steel chair. Former Minnesota state governor, Hollywood actor and former WWE wrestler Jessie 'The Body' Ventura said of wrestling "My advice to anyone thinking of becoming a wrestler is 'be prepared to live in pain for rest of your life'." The highest paid WWE performers are on a wage figure of around $1-2 million a year. The average yearly wage for most wrestlers contracted to WWE would be around the $175,000-$250,000 mark. Their sacrifice for a successful career is more than athletes in most other sports. A footballer might one day need a hip or knee replacement. For a wrestler, there is a real risk of ending up in a wheelchair at an early age. Or worse (between the years 1997 and 2006, sixty-five professional wrestlers died before their fortieth birthday).

The point I'm getting at here is that a wrestler will find it hard to have another career due to these sacrifices. They spend a lot of time on the road travelling from state to state as they work at least four to five times a week in a vast country and also travel to each corner of the globe on world tours. A boxer will sacrifice any form of social life in favour of training to be ready for a big fight. In contrast a footballer will train for two or three hours a day and play one or two games a week. Footballers have plenty of time to study other areas of working life to prepare them for when they retire from football. And what makes some professional footballers think they're important enough to retire from working life altogether in their mid-thirties? The majority of people will have to work well into their sixties before they can retire. There's no reason why a career in football should hold anyone back from doing other things and learning other trades. In the 1970s my uncle was a professional footballer while he studied in his spare-time, eventually taking an economics degree on retirement leading to a new career as a teacher. So the argument that footballers need to earn tens of thousands a week because they will have a short career, isn't a valid one. Especially when some of them talk of too much spare time and boredom (not stupidity and lack of imagination) as being the main reason for blowing hundreds of thousands away on gambling.

The question is whether or not footballers can offer good value for what they earn. The amount of footballers who have earned tens of thousands of pounds per week for very little in return is a list that is too long. Robbie Fowler was a great striker and a likeable, down-to-earth honest character within football, and for that I don't like to criticise him. However, Fowler was on such a high contract at Leeds United, that when he was transferred to Manchester City in 2003, Leeds United were subsidising a percentage of his weekly wage!

Even by 2006 when Robbie Fowler had re-joined Liverpool from Manchester City, Leeds were still paying him a reported weekly wage of £20,000. Hypothetically, had Liverpool played Leeds in the 2005-06 season and had Fowler scored for Liverpool, then Leeds would have been paying a player a weekly salary for scoring against them. Is it me or has football become one big lunatic asylum? It's not just the players who can earn big money for little in return. The men at the FA who negotiated Sven Goran Eriksson's wages should be sedated and restrained to prevent them ever printing out another contract (damn it, too late, they had their hands free to print one out for Steve McClaren!). Long after the 2006 World Cup, Sven Goran Eriksson was receiving £90,000 a week for NOT managing England. With the exception of the current England manager, the rest of the country is not managing England either, so where's our £90,000 a week? Eriksson earned a reported £25 million in wages from his time managing England, and a further £3.2 million for not managing England in a deal that ended in summer 2007, one year after leaving the job as England manager.

In September 2006 Ashley Cole began a successful new career as a stand up comedian, and had the nation in stitches with the "I didn't join Chelsea for the money" gag. Cole left Arsenal after describing the £55,000 he was offered as "taking the piss". He wanted £60,000 a week and when offered only £55,000 Cole claimed that "I nearly swerved the car off the road. I was so incensed. I was trembling with anger." Cole moaned that an extra £5,000 a week was "nothing", even though that figure over the space of a year amounts to £250,000. Ashley Cole's agent was also upset over his client's offer and was reported to have described Cole as "a slave". No doubt that people in the third world who are working in sweatshops for ten pence an hour can also empathise with Cole's rough treatment. It's been over two hundred years since the abolition of the Atlantic slave trade, but it's shameful to learn, that even in this day and age, human beings are being made offers to earn millions of pounds for playing football at their own free will. Why are Amnesty International making such a fuss about things like torture and world poverty, and yet at the same time saying absolutely nothing on the issue of Premiership footballer slavery? When Arsenal offered Cole £55,000 a week it was as if they put him in chains, dragged him on to an overcrowded boat, took him across the ocean in torturous conditions, brutally whipped him and then sold him off to a wealthy landowner who would then work him to death.

When Cole's agent uses the word 'slave' he's referring to the legality of a contract that ties the player to a club, for however many years the player signs on. Once contracted, a player cannot leave without the club's permission or until the contract runs out. Even though in reality, when a player decides he wants to leave a club he is always allowed to go, as managers do not want players who are uncommitted to the club. These contracts are the most valuable asset a footballer has, even though some might complain about restriction of movement. The fact is that footballers can earn incredible sums of money whilst not performing to a decent standard, or in fact not even playing at all. It's what separates them from athletes in other sports whose earnings come about on the basis of how well they perform. Sportsmen such as Tiger Woods and Roger Federer have earned their millions through tournament winnings, appearance money and advertising deals, not weekly contracts where they get paid a fixed fee regardless of the standard of their performance. If they're injured they simply don't get paid. For this reason footballers should consider themselves very lucky and privileged, instead of forever giving the impression that they are hard done by and always worth more than they get. Ashley Cole did in fact receive £60,000 a week in his last season at Arsenal before moving to Chelsea for £90,000 a week. In his last season for Arsenal, Cole spent most of the time laid off with injury and played only a handful of games. Any 'slave' who earns £60,000 a week for not even working isn't doing too badly. And one last thing – since when did slaves have agents?

Stadium designs and identity

A common complaint about Britain today is that every high-street looks the same.

The perception is that no matter what city or town you go to you'll be met with the same shops, the same food chains, the same buildings and a general lack of individual character. This complaint undoubtedly is true.

Before you arrive at any major high-street it's a safe bet that you'll find a McDonalds, Boots, JJB Sports, KFC, Starbucks, Gap, Carphone Warehouse, Clinton Cards, Gregs the baker, Tesco etc. The major brands and chains are now too powerful for anyone else to compete.

Pubs are dominated by major chains such as Wetherspoons, All Bar One, and O'Neil's. Inner city art deco cinemas are being replaced by the out-of-town multiplexes that all look the same, lack romance and show the same choice of mainstream movies. Every bar and nightclub seems to play the same music and serve the same brands of alcohol. In every sector of society individual character seems overwhelmed by a bland one-dimensional vision. Capitalism of this extreme kind is the same as state communism, in that it holds back real choice and individuality.

Football grounds are now losing that individual character. The trend at the moment is for clubs to move into a brand new thirty thousand all-seater stadium and then name the ground after a mobile phone. There is no reason that clubs should feel obliged to stay in the same stadium and never move to a different location. But what's disappointing is that the plans for these new stadiums are all so similar in character, or more to the point, lack of character. It's as if the same design plan gets passed around to every club that moves home. The template for these plans is the Riverside stadium in Middlesbrough which was opened in 1993. It was the first stadium of its kind in England, but it now has many replicas all over the country. The only difference will be either a larger or smaller version of the same stadium and with different coloured seats depending on the team colours of that club. All four sides of the ground are bland and identical, with no features that remotely stand out. These are budget no-frills stadiums with an Asda-like supermarket feel to them. The goalposts and nets themselves now all look the same in every football ground. You might think that sounds trivial but years ago everything about each football ground had an individual touch to it.

Like millions of others I dread living in a world where everything looks and sounds the same. But the people who run our lives believe in this one-vision one-world way of thinking. One of the most iconic and recognisable things about Britain is the double-decker Routemaster bus. However the people in charge of transport in London think that our buses should look like the buses of every other country in Europe. So in replacement of the red double-decker we now have one-level bendy buses that create more congestion, catch fire on a regular basis and quite frankly look crap! When people talk about Britain losing its identity it's usually in a debate over immigration. Yet the people who really take away our identity are the ones who dilute our high streets and destroy our landmarks, usually in the name of money. It wasn't asylum seekers from the Congo who sold off two of my favourite central London pubs to property developers, and turned numerous others into All Bar One style gastro pubs, with white walls and laminate flooring. Nor was it them who put ugly glass panels over a fourteenth century market square in Norwich city centre, or gave planning permission for the unique and world famous Camden Market to be turned into a glass complex shopping mall.

As a consumer I don't want to be presented with the same options every single time I make a journey to the high street. Neither do I want to see the same style stadium every single time I go to watch a game. These new football arenas are a perfect representation of how the British have lost a sense of decor over the years in favour of saving a bit of cash. This country used to care deeply about decoration in the smallest of things, from a street sign, to a lamppost, to a shop front, to a railing. This has unfortunately been replaced with an attitude that ugly street furniture is better for our lives because it's less complicated to make and slightly cheaper. As a result we've been left with many towns and cities that are concrete wastelands.

Many of the clubs who move stadium do so out of trend rather than need. For example Darlington FC in League 2 (the old Fourth Division, former Third Division and the future Starbucks Premiership Minus 3) who moved stadium in 2003. Darlington's highest attendance of all time was just over 20,000 way back in the 1960s. In a good season Darlington's average attendance would be around the 5,000 mark. But bearing in mind Darlington very rarely have a good season their attendance is usually somewhere around the 4,000 figure and that's being generous. In their old stadium Feethams, the ground was right next to the train station and the capacity was around the 8,000 mark. The population of Darlington itself is only 98,000. So naturally the owner of Darlington at the time, George Reynolds, decided that instead of investment in new players, what the club really needed was to go into debt by building a brand new 25,000 out-of-town all-seater stadium. He then named the stadium the Reynolds Arena (no ego trip there!). This was all part of an over-ambitious plan back in 1999 to take Darlington to the Premiership by 2003!

When friends of mine who support Darlington told me about these stadium plans I thought they were just testing me to see how gullible I was. Darlington never have and never will fill this stadium, unless they draw Newcastle United or Manchester United in the FA Cup (or Real Madrid in the Champions League) and rely on the support of the away fans. Even if Darlington were a Premiership team they still wouldn't fill the stadium. The whole idea was about as sensible, practical and necessary as women who shave off their eyebrows and then draw in a thin black line as a replacement. As a result of this crazy location move, Darlo went into administration and George Reynolds left the club (he also had many other reasons to leave the club and was a terrible chairman). The stadium is now named the Balfour Webnet Darlington Arena and the Darlington fans are now left with a stadium that has around 22,000 empty seats every home game. They're probably the only club to have the chant 'NICE GROUND – NO FANS' directed at them each week. When I emailed a friend who supports Darlington, to ask him about life in the new ground, his reply was one that the owners of lower division clubs should take notice of if they have plans to build a new stadium – "*It's rubbish. They've ripped the soul out of the club by moving. I live in Darlo and have only been to about four or five home games this year. In the three and a half years since the move I haven't been once and really enjoyed it. Sitting down, no atmosphere, miles from the pitch, empty ground, no character, £16 for 4th division footy, fans with drums. I'd rather go down the pub and watch the scores come in on the vidiprinter.*"

There are exceptions to this, as some stadiums that have been built in recent years have been practical in meeting attendance demands, whilst also being impressive in structure. Manchester City's Eastlands stadium was built for the Commonwealth games and then given to City in 2003.

It looks okay from the outside, but inside it has a great view from virtually every seat. Bolton Wanderers and Huddersfield Town have modern stadiums from the 1990s that are well designed and original.

Arsenal's new 60,000 Emirates Stadium in Ashburton Grove is one that the jury is still out on. In my opinion, the outside suffers from American city syndrome. It looks great from a distance, but once downtown it feels as if something is missing. It seems to be a combination of grey concrete slabs and glass panels and feels like a mix between old Soviet Bloc brutalism and modern day luxury apartments. It is a good stadium and all it really needs is a lick of red and white paint on the grey concrete slabs to give the place a bit more character. The inside of the stadium is more impressive and has great views and a continental feel to it. It does however lack the special features of Highbury and is also the most unashamedly corporate stadium on the planet, aimed more towards the wealthy than the average fan. It can't claim to be unique in the way Highbury was either, because the Emirates is an exact replica of the Benfica stadium in Lisbon which opened in 2003. All in all though Ashburton Grove is a good place to watch football, and it will be even better once I find the oil fields in Finsbury Park, take the club over and make a few changes.

There is nothing wrong with football clubs moving to new locations, but the move should always be done in a way that maintains a sense of originality, identity and history. Sometimes the better option is to put more money into the current stadium and redevelop. In the 1960s, beautiful Georgian and Victorian homes were seen as outdated and not worth re-developing. As a result they were knocked down and up went tower blocks all over the country. At the time these tower blocks were seen as new and dynamic. Today it is clear that this decision was wrong as tower blocks made many areas of our cities ugly, and more importantly were not good enough for people to live in. You only have to look at the current price of a redeveloped Georgian or Victorian terrace for proof that they had plenty of life in them.

Lack of home-grown players

At the start of the 2006-07 season, 60% of Premiership squad players were not eligible to play for the English national side. During the same period in the Italian Seria A, only 27% of players were not eligible to play for Italy. That statistic alone raised a big debate, not least because England failed miserably in the 2006 World Cup, while Italy won the competition. By the start of the 2007-08 season, in excess of 60% of squad players in the Premiership were not eligible to play for England. That is a dramatic change from the opening day of the first Premiership season in 1992-93, when only eleven players in the whole league were foreigners. Once again, in football we have seen a change that was needed, but one that has gone from one extreme to another.

To complain about the lack of home grown players in the Premiership does not contradict the fact that we also like to see international superstars play for our teams. The best players in the world will always be welcome to play in England. Most of us don't mind the majority of our teams being foreign, as long as they play with skill and commitment. We don't object to foreigners at all, we just don't want to see English players completely shunned. Arsenal have a reputation more than any other for the lack of home -grown players. When Arsenal played Real Madrid in 2006, only two English players were in the starting line-up. That's the starting line-up of Real Madrid by the way. Arsenal didn't field one Englishman (though we did field two Spaniards which was nearly as many as Real Madrid). When a top team like Arsenal does not field any English players, then it has to be damaging to the national side. But this is not Arsene Wenger's fault. It is not his obligation to field an Arsenal team on the basis of helping the English national team. If he feels that his best eleven are foreigners, then that is the team he should start with.

It is hard to argue with Wenger when he says "Sport is competition. Competition is based on merit." If having too many overseas players in the Premiership is damaging to the national team, then the governing bodies of English football are the ones who should be calling for changes.

In 2007 Sepp Blatter, of all people, decided to do the talking on behalf of the England manager. He proposed bringing in laws that would limit the number of foreigners in the European leagues. The Premier League response was very hostile to this proposal.

Every single quote from the Premier League spokesman, made it clear that they would be against any form of limitations on overseas players. Of course, why should the Premier League (who have three out of twelve representatives on the FA board) give a damn about the English national side? The Premier League is run by the Premiership club themselves. Their prime concern is making money, and luckily for them, people are very quick to forget history. In Chapter two, I said that the reason for the formation of the Premier League was to re-brand football, make the game more commercially viable and to generate more money for the top clubs. Well there was actually another reason given for its formation, one which most people appear to have forgotten about. The FA claimed that the introduction of the Premier League would benefit the England team. A statement in 1991 from the FA told us that *"The prospect of success for the England team would, at once, be enhanced."* Enhanced how? The last time England progressed so far as a World Cup semi-final was in 1990, two years before the formation of the Premier League.

Since then following England has been one disappointment after another. At the time of writing, England have failed to qualify for the 2008 European Championship, having lost to both Russia and Croatia, and failing to beat those heavyweights of world football – Israel and Macedonia. Oh well, I suppose that just the one failure in the Premier League master plan isn't too bad going. Why be upset by the continued underachievement of the England team, when the Premiership clubs are selling so many more replica shirts and corporate packages? Cheer up England fans, because even though our much-hyped, much-pampered, overpaid, gutless, team of prima donnas can't even qualify for a tournament, our Premier League stands alone as the money-making champion of world football. Eat your hearts out Europe.

Limitations on foreign players are likely to face problems from beaurocratic EU working laws. For a proposal to stand a chance of being made law, it would need strong support from bodies like the Premier League and the FA. A proposal perhaps along these lines: *A team must have in the starting line up, at least three players who are eligible to play for the country in which the domestic league is based.* I made that one up myself, but I don't think it's too harsh. If anything, I think that a lot of fans would prefer a law that goes way further than just three players. One ruling that did get passed in 2006, was a law that required every team in Europe to have at least two squad players that have come up from the clubs' youth academies. But due to the nature of this law, foreign players can be included in this, just as long as they've spent two years at the club before they reach the age of twenty-one. For example, Cesc Fabregas at Arsenal would, under this law, be classed as a home-grown player, because he signed from Barcelona when he was sixteen. The biggest worry for the future of the England national team, is that many youth academies are now dominated by young foreign players.

The crazy nature of the transfer market is the main reason why a club like Arsenal reject English players in favour of foreigners. English players are so heavily overpriced, and with little justification. Foreign players simply offer better value for money and have brought success to a club like Arsenal. The question of why English players are so expensive has never been answered. Let's face it, when Thierry Henry gets sold for the same amount as Darren Bent (£17 million), then we know that the percentage of foreign players in the Premiership will continue to get higher with every new season.

<u>Football phone-ins</u>

So what's my problem with these audio fan forums such as Radio Five's *606* and the numerous shows on TalkSPORT? In principle I like the idea. Fans get the opportunity to voice their opinions on live radio. The problem is that some of the presenters and fans that take part tend to be the kind of people who need to get out more and do something different in their lives. In football phone-ins there appears to be only one thing wrong with football, and that one thing is referees. When listening to phone-in shows it makes it even harder to understand why on earth any sane person would aspire to be a referee or linesman. These fans and presenters get so angry at a human error by a man who's trying to be neutral in a very difficult and pressured environment. How bored must you be on a Saturday evening to feel the urge to phone up Radio Five and complain about a 'wrong' offside decision? I'm not saying I've never been angry at a referee or shouted at the man with the whistle if I think he's wrong. Yet when I shout at the official it is spur of the moment, irrational, biased, and it's not personal. A couple of hours after the game I won't feel the need to phone up national radio and bore the whole country about a handball that wasn't given.

The presenters encourage this berating of referees on a weekly basis. I'd like to see these radio hosts try and referee a Sunday league match at Hackney Marshes between two unfit pub sides in a slow-paced game, let alone a fast-paced professional game. They'd last about ten minutes before being chased off the field by former felons and escaping to the car park. I once refereed a match between two under-sixteen school teams. I thought I did a pretty good job and got most decisions right, but it taught me that to get every decision right as a referee is impossible because you just can't see everything that's going on. A player isn't expected to have a 100% pass rate throughout a match, so why is a referee expected to spot every handball or every foul? These people are only human.

A lot of these radio presenters can hardly be described as sporting experts. Let me give you some names of people who have presented football phone-ins in recent years: David Mellor, Richard Littlejohn, Gary Newbon and Mike Parry. Former Conservative MP David Mellor was one of the first hosts of a radio phone-in show and presented the *606* show on BBC Five Live. I've heard Mellor present a good show for classic FM, but to let him run a football show was a bad idea because he's not in touch with most supporters. He could never seem to understand fans like myself who don't want to sit down in quiet for the entire game. He was replaced by Richard Littlejohn who's just a bad idea in general. Littlejohn is an unpleasant bigot who is also the only person in the country to see no irony in his catchphrase '*You couldn't make it up.*' Richard Littlejohn can feel free to sue me for calling him an 'unpleasant bigot' but I have more than enough evidence to back that up. His newspaper articles and TV shows portray a man devoid of any wit, charm, common sense or objectivity.

Gary Newbon presents phone-in shows for TalkSPORT radio and Sky television. If you were to shoot him for being a football expert you'd be gunning down an innocent man. Like Mellor, I think he's also completely out of touch with many fans. I recall one show Gary Newbon hosted when a Chelsea fan phoned in to talk about the rising cost of following his team. The fan complained that he had forked out well over £100 to take his young son to a Chelsea game. Newbon's response was along the lines of "Don't come on here and tell me about how much you had to pay to watch your team. This is a football show. I'm not here to talk about how expensive your ticket is." Charming! My question to Gary Newbon therefore would be – when was the last time you paid money to go to a football match? Pundits and journalists who work in football, do not have to pay to gain access to football stadiums. Maybe if he did have to pay for tickets, and were on an average wage, then it might dawn on him that ticket pricing in football is an issue for some people.

One of the most popular phone-ins in recent times has been TalkSPORT's weekday morning show that was presented by Alan Brazil and Mike Parry. It was second only to Classic FM in ratings for commercial radio. The good thing about this show was that it dealt with a range of subjects that even included wider news issues when there were more important things to talk about than sport. Big boned host Mike 'Porky' Parry talks a lot of rubbish and is well known for it. For example, he once suggested removing September 11th from the calendar because it holds bad memories! He also advocated that British footballers wear Union Jack armbands in support of the Iraq war! Despite his obvious flaws, he does have an entertainment value. He's thick-skinned enough to accept it when callers phone in and recommend that he goes back to the mug-farm.

In late 2005 I was in a bar in London's Haymarket during a night of Champions League football. It turned out that Mike Parry and Alan Brazil were also there on a promotion night. A friend and I were approached by a good-looking hostess who invited us to the VIP section to join them – if we paid £30 for the privilege. I declined, giving the reason that "There's a chance I might strangle Mike Parry if I get to close to him and he chooses to speak." The offer then went down to £15 (no joke) but we still didn't take it. However, we ended up watching a TV screen that was situated right next to the TalkSPORT VIP section where Mike Parry and Alan Brazil were hosting this promotion night. There were TV screens all over the bar but that didn't hold the interest of Parry or Brazil who make a living out of giving their 'expert' opinions on football. They spent the whole first half eating chicken wings from the buffet and sipping champagne. They certainly were not paying any attention to the night's Champions League action, which would not be a criticism if they didn't then have the audacity to present a show live from the bar at half-time with their 'expert' opinions of the night's football. Mike Parry got the show started by saying "Going from the first half it's clear that Manchester

United are not the same team without Wayne Rooney." Those of us near the VIP section looked at each other with disbelief, our main thought being that how dare this man preach an opinion on something he didn't even bother watching. A friend of mine was so incensed that he got as close as he could to the radio stage and yelled out some advice to Parry which was along the lines of "Why don't you shut the fuck up you prick!" To his credit, Mike Parry didn't take the comment too badly and jokingly waved his fist towards my friend. Unfortunately the bouncers did take it badly and the night ended early!

Radio phone-in shows have certainly not been without entertaining moments. My favourite ever call was from a Chelsea fan on TalkSPORT who complained that "It's all very well having all these posh Herberts at Chelsea these days. But what about the likes of me who like to organise a fight before a football match!" Another call I remember fondly was after Arsenal beat Spurs 3-0 in a North London derby. Gary Newbon was the presenter that day and it went something along these lines:

Caller – Terrible day today mate. Totally outplayed by the Gooners. I hate to admit it but Arsenal are in a different league to us at the moment.

Newbon – Bad day for Tottenham.

Caller – I blame my old man for taking me down White Hart Lane all them years ago and making me a Tottenham fan. As a result of that my life's been a misery. Nothing but hurt.

Newbon – Well thanks for the call. And maybe things will get better for Spurs.

Caller – Oh one last thing. Tottenham are mugs. I'm really a Gooner… Aaahhhaaa (loud cheers from people in the background).

Caller hangs up.

Newbon – Well that's very clever. I'm sure you're very proud of yourself. Can we have some serious calls please.

So in principle the phone-in show is a good idea and I always like to hear other people's opinions on sport and world issues. This should really be on the list of positives, and with a better range of callers and a few less obnoxious hosts, it could be.

Lack of free speech

"I disapprove of what you say, but I will defend to the death your right to say it"

Voltaire

Footballer interviews are now as interesting as John Major discussing car insurance with James Blunt. Players seemed to have mastered the art of talking at length but not really saying anything. Young players are now even trained by their agents on how to give interviews in the most mundane and robotic-like way. In fact, I wonder if footballers are now so used to speaking in this emotionless way, that they do so even when not on camera? Perhaps a conversation in their private life would sound a bit like this…

Frank's wife – Frank, you are by far the best lover I've ever had.

Frank Terry – It was a very encouraging performance. Being a good lover yourself, it meant that there was that added pressure tonight, but I dug in, went in hard and put in that extra effort. Hopefully that should leave me full of confidence for the next love-making session.

It must be weird living with these guys. However, at least it would mean the average footballer could stay mentally strong, even in the face of a crisis…

Frank's wife – Oh Frank (starts to sob). I'm so sorry you had to lose an arm in that car accident.

Frank Terry – Well it's never easy to lose an arm, but hopefully another one will bounce back shortly. I'm certainly not panicking and nor is the doctor.

I'd recommend therapy for these guys, but I'm not sure how successful it would be…

Psychotherapist – Frank, you have been diagnosed with a condition that represses charisma and prevents an individual from expressing his true feelings. How does that make you feel?

Frank Terry – Well there are no easy conditions to be diagnosed with. Obviously it's not the outcome I would have wanted, however I'm positive that by this time next week I will have turned it around. We've just got to take each session as it comes.

Can we start allowing these guys to talk from the heart please? Not that there is an official rule in football banning people from speaking openly. But to quote a lyric from a Clash song *'You have the right to free speech. Just don't be dumb enough to actually try it'.* The culprits in this case, are certain sections of the media who can twist people's words, and also the FA who can hand out fines for what they perceive as improper conduct. In 2004, Arsene Wenger was fined under the FA Rule E3 for improper conduct after saying "We know how Ruud van Nistelrooy behaves. He can only cheat people – we know him very well." Okay, that was not very flattering towards Ruud van Nistelrooy. But it was Wenger's feelings at the time, and he probably had at least some justification for saying those words. He honestly thought that van Nistelrooy was a cheat. Of course the FA would rather Wenger's comments were along the lines of "Well I think Ruud went down a bit easy. There didn't appear to be any contact. Obviously we're very disappointed with the outcome." BORING! And not only is it boring, it is also dishonest. That is not what we as football supporters wants to hear.

The FA and Premier League seem to be terrified of anything that doesn't fit in with their safe and conformist image of football. They view disagreement and conflict as a bad advert for football, which couldn't be further from reality. Arsene Wenger and Alex Ferguson have both been brought to answer to the FA for having a so-called 'war of words', even though this sort of rivalry is what both the supporters and media enjoy as part of the entertainment of the game. During his time in English football, Jose Mourinhio was a breath of fresh air, because he's a man who let's you know what he thinks – not what other people want him to say. Nowadays, if a manager criticises a referee in a post-match interview, he then opens himself up to possible disciplinary action. I don't like to see managers blame the referee for a defeat when it's usually their own players' bad performance that is to blame. But surely they have the right to voice an honest opinion without having to answer to the FA?

Football television coverage is now censored and certain clips are even banned from being broadcast. The authorities have actually gone so far as to ban the infamous clip of when Eric Cantona karate kicked a Crystal Palace fan in 1995.

Again, this incident is censored because it sends out a 'negative' image of football. This is ridiculous because that incident was dramatic, and drama is the basis of a sport like football. Nobody got killed or even seriously hurt, and if a lot of people are honest, then that karate kick from Cantona to that gobby Palace fan was, at the very least, intriguing television. During that same week, TV presenter and Stoke City fan Nick Hancock was asked his opinion on the Cantona incident – *"I thought it was disgraceful, I thought it was shameful, I thought it was disgusting, but most of all, I thought it was very very funny. Easily the best thing to have happened all season."* Hancock summed it up perfectly. However, we're all supposed to pretend that we hate to see this kind of incident happen.

These moments of controversy should be put into some sort of perspective. When you consider that at one time, thousands of people attended spectator sports in which lions ripped human beings to shreds, and gladiators slew one another, one isolated karate kick from a poetic Frenchman was hardly going to destroy the fabric of a game like football. I admit to being a hypocrite when it comes to the morals of the game. On the one hand I love to see football played with good sportsmanship and by gentlemen with integrity. But on the other hand, I also love the side of the game that brings up bad behaviour and heated rivalry. But all these things, whether moral or immoral, are what makes sport so interesting and makes us love it. Not everyone wants to live in the superficial world that the FA and Premier League like to promote. Maybe football's men in suits have been taking some image advice from the politicians? For example, the government have tried to ban one man from protesting outside Parliament about the Iraq war – because they believe it sends out a bad impression of Britain to tourists! Protester, Brian Haw, has staged a one man protest on the pavement of Parliament Square since the war began, and displays a number of anti-war flags and banners. His right to do this gives tourists a very good impression of our country, in terms of the freedom to stage a protest directly outside the most influential building in the country. Though according to the Government, when tourists see his protest they turn to one-another and say "Well honey, that's the last time I'm ever going to visit London."

Whether it is words or symbols, what is being repressed is a simple freedom of expression. At the Emirates Stadium, national flags are now banned in the stands, for fear of causing offence. As an Arsenal fan, I would like to inform the club, that I would not be the least bit offended by, for example, a Nigerian flag that reads 'Lagos Arsenal Supporters Club'. If you market yourselves as a club that welcomes people of all nations, then don't ban the whole world from bringing their flags into the stadium.

This all supposedly came about because of a dispute between London based Greek and Turkish Cypriots. Some Greek Cypriots were upset because some Turkish Cypriots had brought their flag into the Emirates, which is a flag that is not recognised by the UN. Because of this dispute, Arsenal thought it best to ban everyone from bringing a national flag into the stadium, which, it could be argued, shows disregard for the other 99.9% of Arsenal fans who have nothing to do with these differences.

Greek Cypriots are understandably very passionate over the illegal occupation of a region of their country, and perhaps Arsenal should have just banned national flags that are not recognised by the UN. But let's look at this from another angle. How would it go down at the football club Apollen Limassol, if all Cypriot national flags were banned from their stadium, because Northern Irish Catholics were unhappy about the flag of Ulster being displayed in the stands?

The attack on free speech has even gone beyond what the football authorities see fit to deal with. In 2005, Aussie midfielder Harry Kewell took Gary Lineker to the High Court in a lawsuit about remarks Lineker had made in the *Daily Telegraph*. His case against Lineker was no deeper than the fact that Lineker had said Kewell's transfer to Liverpool had made him "ashamed" of football. This was hardly a controversial opinion from Lineker, as Harry Kewell's transfer to Liverpool showed us how much money certain elements in the game (i.e. agents) make out of player transfers. Harry Kewell joined Liverpool from Leeds for £5 million in 2003. Of the £5 million transfer fee, £2 million went to the company Max-sport which is run by Kewell's personal manager Bernie Madic.

The transfer, although legally sound, deserved to be more than just questioned, and I'm being careful with my words just in case. Mr Kewell and his personnel are in the litigation mood. His transfer to Liverpool showed fans that their hard earned money goes out of football and into the pockets of people who have too much influence in the way the game is run. Of course his transfer to Liverpool was shameful – end of story. What would Kewell rather Lineker have said? *"The £2 million pounds that went out of the game and into Max-sport's bank account was a true credit to football. It just makes me feel ashamed that it didn't happen when I was playing."* In the end, the judge in the case came to no conclusion so neither side won a victory. If Kewell had won this case, then it would have not just been damaging to what people in football can say, but also damaging to the opinions expressed by those outside the law of football. Could a journalist get sued every time he or she referred to a player's performance as lazy or poor etc?

Oh by the way, speaking of those certain elements in football who make so much money out of the game...

Player agents

"The major problem is not bungs – my major problem is paying agents full stop. They work on behalf of the player and I don't understand why the club has to pay them as well."

Mike Newell

During the 1980s and 1990s two words helped give agents a negative image within the game:

1. Eric
2. Hall

Yes Eric Hall, remember that guy? The cigar chomping celebrity agent with an 'endearing lisp'. Eric once said that what makes America a better country than Britain is that "When Americans see you in a Rolls Royce they say 'Hey that guy's a winner'. When the Brits see you in a Rolls Royce they want to scratch it." You're wrong Eric, there is a simple explanation for why this happens. If you've found that people want to scratch your Rolls Royce or stick two fingers up at you, it's simply because you're inside it. The Americans don't know who you are, luckily for them. They've got guns out there Eric, so I suggest you keep it that way.

Another thing Eric Hall once said on the Saint and Greavsie talk show in 1995 was "What's wrong with managers taking bungs? I don't see the problem." The problem is simple. If an agent offers a manager a backhander to sign a player then that signing can have no credibility. Everyone will see that signing not as a vital addition to the team, but simply as someone brought in by the manager for his own financial gain. In January 2006 former Luton Town manager Mike Newell said that he had been offered bungs and that he was prepared to name names of corrupt agents. He was backed up by former QPR manager Ian Holloway who also claimed to have been offered a bung. After these allegations the general consensus from commentators, former managers and players is that agent bungs are commonplace within football and have been for a number of years. Former football agent Steven Noel Hill has even claimed that if his experience is anything to go by "80% of deals have bungs attached to them." In September 2006 the BBC aired an undercover documentary that aimed to expose this type of corruption within the game. Sam Allardyce was at the centre of the allegations and it was claimed that he received illegal payments from agents via his son, who was one of three hundred licensed football agents in England. The programme itself was considered by many as over-hyped, lacking in substance and a damp squib. Yet one thing it highlighted very clearly was how easy it was to do a bung deal and get away with it. This is because any illegal money transfers would either be made in cash, or paid into a Swiss bank account making it untraceable.

Anyone who is corrupt would have learnt a lesson off George Graham who was found guilty of taking a bung in 1995. Graham accepted a payment of £425,000 from agent Rune Hauge for the signing of Pal Lyderson in 1992. Graham was investigated when the Inland Revenue started to ask questions about the £425,000 that went into his bank account undeclared. George Graham claimed, in his defence that the money was given to him as a gift and a thank you (in other words a bung!). But what was interesting was that Lyderson made no impact at Arsenal and played very few games. This scandal cost Graham his job at Arsenal and he was banned from football for two years. The BBC documentary was shortly followed by a report from Lord Stevens that looked into corruption in football. Stevens found suspicion in thirty-nine transfer dealings which was 10% of what he was asked to investigate.

After all these allegations focusing on bungs, agents were understandably on the defensive, with the main line of defence being "There are a few bad apples, but most agents do a good job for their clients." Agents can get away with claiming that they do a good job for their clients, but one thing you'll never hear an agent have the audacity to claim is "I do a good job for football." Bung scandals and corruption are no doubt damaging for football, but it is what agents are allowed to get away with legally which is the real scandal. When we as fans purchase a football ticket, a percentage of that money will go to players' agents. There are actually no official figures for how much Premiership clubs pay to agents each financial year. This is because the clubs usually refuse to release the figures of these payments. Manchester United released the details of their agent payments in 2005 and the figure was £2.2 million. £1.2 million alone went to one agency for the sale of Wayne Rooney from Everton in 2004. When, Manchester United were bought out by Malcolm Glazer and taken off the stock exchange, they no longer had an obligation to release these figures and stopped doing so from 2005.

The highest ever disclosed fee to have been negotiated by a player agent was the figure of £3 million to Pini Zahavi, for his handling in Yakubu Aiyegbeni's £7.5 million transfer to Middlesbrough in January 2007. The full £3 million depended on Yakubu staying at Middlesbrough for five years, which he didn't, having moved on to Everton for £11.2 million in August 2007.

But don't cry to hard for Pini, because another transfer deal will always result in yet another payment for the player's agent. It would appear to many, that this is simply money going out of football and into the hands of people whose sole interest in the game is to exploit it. If there's one thing that brings both the fans and clubs together, it's the shared loathing of player agents. It could be argued, that those of us who dislike player agents, would probably be represented by one if we were footballers. Like them or loath them, they're the ones with the power to get their clients the best possible wage deal. Well that's the perception, but there are arguments and evidence to the contrary. Robbie Fowler became one of Britain's wealthiest footballers by using a financial adviser as opposed to an agent. Gary Neville is one of very few players to have spoken out against player agents "They [footballers] think they need them [agents] but it's not the case. They need good advice and good accountants. Not people who are going to take hundreds of thousands of pounds off them." Agents are most likely to make their main income from a commission, based on a percentage of their client's earnings. Rio Ferdinand famously had a pay dispute with Manchester United before the 2005-06 season. It was reported that he felt his wages should rise from £100,000 a week to £120,000 a week. It was alleged that the extra £20,000 a week would then pay his agent's commission. So an agent can possibly get £20,000 a week just through representing one player. Shouldn't examples such as this make fans sit up and think about where their hard earned money goes? If the commission Rio Ferdinand's agent earns per week is indeed £20,000, then that's more than many people earn in a year of hard graft.

Media scrutiny

"If you are able to play football really well you will be a player in the top division. If you play football badly you will be a second rate player. If you can't play at all then surely you will be a journalist."

Johan Cruyff

Journalism is a noble profession and a free media is essential to living in a free society. Great journalism can be responsible for giving us knowledge, raising awareness, exposing corruption and even saving lives. So to put all the media in the same category is very unfair. Richard Littlejohn and David Attenborough both work in the media, but they couldn't be further apart in manners, intellect, charm and talent. The tabloids themselves have some excellent writers and great journalism is still alive. However, there are too many hacks out there who are putting their profession to shame and dragging it through the mud and into the gutter. Sensationalist sports reporting is not a new thing that has sprung up since the formation of the Premiership. But reporting in certain sections of the media has become even more ridiculous, vicious and over the top.

With footballers being such highly paid media stars, they now appear in newspapers and magazines on a regular basis in trivial and tedious gossip stories. It's part of a culture that has made household names of non-personalities simply because they date footballers. Having an affair with David Beckham is enough to make a girl a household celebrity name and earn millions as a result. It's crazy to think that most people in Britain are probably more likely to have heard of Rebecca Loos than the Magna Carta.

Wayne Rooney's girlfriend Coleen McLoughlin, is reported to be worth £5 million a year through her celebrity status gained through dating a footballer. £5 million a year for having no recognisable talent other than shopping is great work if you can get it and good luck to her. It certainly doesn't make her the fool if magazines pay her good money because their readers want to read about her life. In summer 2006, seventeen-year-old Theo Walcot was chosen to be in England's World Cup squad for Germany. Before that he was unknown outside of football, but his surprise inclusion to the England squad put him on the front pages and he was soon hailed by the press as the new Wayne Rooney. The very next day, his sixteen-year-old girlfriend was on the front pages of the tabloids and by the following weekend one newspaper was already running 'World Exclusives' about her sex life. Within one day of being 'famous', people in the media were saying that this girl could be worth millions. A sixteen-year-old girl, who nobody had heard of, who nobody had heard speak, who nobody knew as having any talent, can be worth millions just for being blonde and dating a footballer. I know they say that it's too easy to be famous these days but this is just crazy. Time to bring in the men in white coats (and check out their girlfriends for any hidden talents, they might be worth millions for being able to breathe).

The 2006 World Cup coverage itself was dominated by the wives and girlfriends of the England players, as certain papers carried fascinating stories of how they went out of the hotel room and did some shopping. Girls with lots of money going shopping – who would have thought!

During this period, *The Sun* columnist and professional bigot John Gaunt even had the audacity to criticise *The Independent* newspaper for devoting an entire front page to the problem of 4x4 cars and the threat to the environment they carry. Of course John Gaunt is spot on as ever. The issue of global warming is totally trivial compared to the 'Wags' shopping habits, and these muesli-eating tree huggers at *The Independent* should do more to raise awareness on real issues, just like *The Sun* does.

Many believe that football has become too high pressured and demanding. In the back pages of newspapers, manager and player quotes are now as heavily scrutinised as those of politicians. There is certainly no shortage of media spin, plus a misrepresentation of quotes that are all too common in political coverage. *The Sun* in particular offers a very aggressive confrontational style to its sports reporting. They decide what someone has said to fit the story they want to sell. For example they once had a back page with a picture of Arsene Wenger along with the headline:

YOU MUGS: WENGER SLAMS OVERSPENDING CHELSEA

One important thing was missing from this headline: quotation marks either side of the words 'you mugs'. No doubt the reason these quotation marks were not there was because Wenger didn't actually use these words (unless this was the Arsene Wenger that starred in the Football Factory). *The Sun* newspaper were the ones calling Chelsea 'mugs', but the way they presented the story made Arsene Wenger look like the aggressor. Wenger's actual words were along the lines of "Chelsea spend over the odds for players." Hardly an outrageous accusation. If anything Wenger was being very polite in explaining why it's so hard to compete with Chelsea and yet he's made to sound disrespectful.

One of countless other misrepresentations like this one, had another back page picture of Arsene Wenger along with the headline: **WE DON'T FEAR CHELSEA.** Again no quotation marks, yet the paper manipulates the reader in to thinking that these are Wenger's words. In reading the article it's clear that Wenger did not even mention Chelsea. When looking for the quotation marks his actual words were along the lines of "I still think that Manchester United are the main threat to us this season." In bold I've put an example of the kind of headlines that feature on the back pages of tabloid newspapers. Below the headline is an example of what the player or manager is more likely to have said.

I'LL SAVE CITY FROM THE DROP
"We've got nine games to avoid relegation. I'll do all I can to help City get maximum points in those nine games."

YOU'RE A BUNCH OF LOSERS
"United have lost a lot of games this season which proves they're beatable."

I'D RATHER LYON WIN THE CHAMPIONS LEAGUE THAN CHELSEA.

"I've got great respect for the Lyon manager from my time working with him. For this reason I hope they can go all the way and win the Champions League."

WE'LL SMASH THE HAMMERS

"We're confident we can go to West Ham and get three points."

I'LL SHOOT US TO WORLD CUP GLORY

"I think we stand a good chance of winning the World Cup"

YOU SLAGS! WE'RE GOING TO BURN DOWN YOUR HOUSES, RAPE ALL YOUR WOMEN, EAT YOUR CHILDREN AND THEN PISS ON YOUR GRAVES. LET'S 'AVE IT

"We're looking forward to going up there and getting stuck in."

Okay, so football interviews are boring and the media are looking for more bite to create interest in a headline. But that's still no excuse to misrepresent what someone has actually said.

Some people in the media claim that footballers should act as positive role models for children. But a hospital visit from a footballer to sick patients will not find a place in the back pages of the newspapers, and footballers do this sort of thing more than people think. Before a friend of mine's baby girl died in hospital, the ward got a visit from none other than Thierry Henry, Robert Pires and Patrick Vieira.

This kind of gesture means a lot to people and because it doesn't create any headlines proves that the footballers who make these visits do so for honourable reasons. Stories about footballers' sex lives won't make it to the back pages either. No, they're far more likely to be on the front page instead, beside the heading WORLD EXCLUSIVE. No doubt that these world exclusives cause plenty of controversy and debate in places like Sudan, Paraguay and Fiji. If positive headlines don't sell then it leaves those in the public eye in a total no-win situation.

The newspapers expect footballers to be good role models because they hold such a high profile. But newspapers also hold a high profile in society.

Why are the tabloid newspapers not expected to act as role models? Every day millions of people read these papers, including children. Surely then journalists have as much responsibility as anyone else in public life to show integrity and pride in their profession. However, it does seems that the example some newspapers send out to kids is this:

1. Betrayal is fine. It's okay to pay someone for a kiss and tell story.
2. It's okay to tell lies about people and misrepresent the facts.
3. Character assassination is okay in order to make money.
4. It's okay to be rude, biased and un-objective.
5. Racial stereotyping of other nations is acceptable.
6. It's also acceptable to then run headlines of shock and disgust when the same racial stereotyping is displayed by English football fans whilst in other countries.
7. It's right to condemn a celebrity for paying a hooker for sex. However by all means pay the same hooker a four figure sum for that 'World Exclusive'.
8. We must make people feel bad about their bodies through over-fussy and obscene scrutiny – and that it's moral to show a twenty-year-old girl in a bikini under the headline 'Cellulite Church' (Charlotte Church).

9. It's okay to kick people when they're down. Show no mercy. When someone's going through a painful time make the pain even worse and stick that boot in.

The excuse that hacks always give is that they are simply giving the public what they want. Yet that is about the worst and most shameful line of defence that any self-respecting journalist can give, because their job should be about truth and integrity, not cheap pandering to the lowest common denominator. Do these people have any pride in their profession? Unfortunately this sort of journalist doesn't seem to be accountable to anyone. If a footballer brings his profession in to disrepute then he will be fined and banned by the football authorities. Newspapers will just get a slap on the wrist from the Press Complaints Commission.

Maybe journalists should be given a three-month ban from reporting, or even given a fine for every time they tell a porky. Some newspapers will happily tolerate a journalist who lies, just so long as those lies are selling more papers. Even if a lie means the newspaper gets sued, there's still a good chance they would have made more money from sales as a result of the lie and subsequent publicity. So when a newspaper pays a "slapper" money to tell all about a one-night stand she had with a footballer, ask yourself one important question, who is really setting the nation a bad example?

Interpretation and rankings

I always thought that football was a game in which the winner was decided when one team scores more goals than the other. I've just checked Wikipedia and apparently this still is the case. So what's this obsession from the television and newspapers for giving players marks out of ten? Near the end of every England game John Motson will ask his co-commentator "So how many marks out of ten for England?" The nation then holds it's breath as a positive score from Mark Lawrenson of around the eight to ten mark will unleash scenes of mass joy and celebration. Marks out of ten are for things like ice dancing, gymnastics and dog shows. Football is not down to interpretation, it's down to goals. So cut it out!

FIFA currently have world rankings which are a complete waste of time. Again it's all down to interpretation which is not what a sport like football is about.

A country might boast about their team having a high FIFA ranking but actually it's meaningless. Even if these rankings are based on results it's still meaningless, as some countries will play more challenging fixtures than others. Mexico and USA regularly have a high FIFA ranking, because most of the internationals they play are against very weak opposition. These were the FIFA top ten rankings that were decided before the World Cup in 2006:

1. Brazil
2. Czech Republic
3. Holland
4. Mexico
5. USA
6. Spain
7. Portugal
8. France
9. Argentina
10. England

Before World Cup 2006, the USA were considered the fifth best team in the world! A team that couldn't make it through the first group stage and didn't expect to either. They finished well below Italy who did not even feature in this top ten FIFA ranking, and who by the way won the World Cup. These rankings are pointless because they're based on a country's performance over a period of time and not how good a team currently is.

For example, a team could be rated highly in 2008 partly because they performed well in 2006. But even if the rankings were based on more recent form, who's to say that the Czech Republic are better than Spain, or that Mexico are better than Argentina? For a realistic and more accurate pointer to the best teams in the world, I would suggest looking at the bookmakers betting odds before a major tournament (unless you're a gambling addict in which case try and find a less expensive hobby).

Okay a slightly trivial negative to bring up, but I felt it was worth a mention. Unlike the next and final negative which is a cancer on the whole of football.

Prawn sandwiches

All the negatives points about football that have been mentioned, can be linked back to one thing and one thing alone. The problems in football have nothing really to do with agents, directors, advertisers or anything else. It all comes down to one deadly evil. The manufacturers of a perverse seafood sandwich carry with them the guilt of destroying the very fabric of the game. Speak to any disillusioned supporter in the country, and they will tell you that the main problem with football today – is the 'prawn sandwich brigade'.

It is scientifically proven that prawn sandwiches harm the voice box so severely that the vocal capacity is damaged, resulting in the lack of atmosphere at football grounds. The prawn sandwich also acts as a sedative which turns people from partisans into passive souls without emotion or expression.

If you go to any football ground in the country you will see prawn sandwich sellers in the stadium and outside on the street. Just before half-time fans will sneak out of the game to buy a prawn sandwich before the queue gets too long. These prawn sandwich stalls and bars were introduced as a form of kryptonite to keep away scum from football stadiums. Gone are the days when football fans stuffed their fat faces with burgers, bagels, pies and hot dogs. That just doesn't happen at football anymore. Football fans are healthy eaters, who would never dream of paying over the odds for a piece of watered-down meat in a bap. Well I've done my research. I went down to my local Budgens just to see how expensive, elitist and up-their-own-arse these prawn sandwich tyrants really are, compared to the more down to earth sandwich types.

Bacon lettuce & Tomato	**£2.09**
Egg Mayonnaise & Bacon	**£2.09**
All day breakfast sandwich	**£2.09**
Chicken Salad	**£2.09**
Chicken Tikka	**£2.09**
Ham & Pickle	**£1.59**
Cheese & Tomato	**£1.59**
Prawn & Mayo	**£1.49**

Okay, so they're not actually that expensive. Perhaps we should focus our attention on the *'Egg Mayonnaise & Bacon Brigade'* as being ruinous of football. But for now at least, prawn sandwiches remain the problem. So to all you fishermen and prawn manufacturers out there – I hope you're satisfied with what you've done to our game. But I do have a confession to make that destroys all credibility to this book and exposes me as a fraud in my belief that football should be the game of the people. I think prawn sandwiches actually taste quite nice.

Okay I'll get my jacket...

Chapter 10
The model...

"By the turn of the millennium West Ham United will have won twenty league championships."

Nostradamus

Many claim that the English Premiership is the best football league in the world. It's by far the richest, but the case for being the world's greatest league should certainly not be judged on wealth. Other people will make the case for the Italian or Spanish leagues as being superior. Either way, the three top football leagues in the world have always been considered those in England, Spain and Italy. But is this judged on fan attendance or entertainment? If success is judged on pulling in numbers through the turnstiles, then the statistics emphatically favour the German Bundesliga, which in recent years has boasted the highest average in crowd attendance in Europe.

The German Bundesliga has always been in the shadow of the English, Spanish and Italian leagues. There's no doubt that in terms of players, the Bundesliga does not attract anywhere near the number of world superstars that its rivals do. So in that sense it's somewhat surprising that the Bundesliga will average 4,000 more fans a week per game than its nearest challenger, the English Premiership. But it does prove that to bring true football fans through the turnstiles you don't necessarily need £100,000 a week superstars. The success of the German Bundesliga is very simple. Their stadiums are brilliantly well designed and original as was showcased in the 2006 World Cup. The standard of Bundesliga football is high despite the lack of world superstars, and the price of a ticket is around €10 euros.

But there is one glaring drawback with the German league – one which they share with the other top leagues in Europe. That is the lack of competition on the field. Bayern Munich are Germany's richest club, and have dominated the Bundesliga for much of the past two decades. Between 1986 and 2006 they won twelve league championships. In Europe, the teams who spend the most – win the most – case closed. The dominance of a select few is bad for sport, as excitement in a game like football doesn't come through fancy footwork or even a high scoring game.

The excitement in football comes through high tension and drama. A low scoring game can be thrilling simply because of the tension of the occasion. Take for example the time when Arsenal beat Liverpool 2-0 at Anfield in 1989 in one of the most spectacular games ever.

The night when the league championship was decided on goal difference with the last kick of the season from Michael Thomas. The greatest game I ever attended was when Manchester United beat Arsenal 2-1 at Villa Park in the 1999 FA Cup semi-final. Ryan Giggs scored a great solo goal in the second half of extra time to take United through to the final. Dennis Bergkamp had earlier missed a penalty in the last minute of normal time that would have taken Arsenal through to the final. It was a horrible result and a hard defeat to take. But it was the most competitive, evenly matched, adrenalin-filled night of football that I have been a part of. A 3-3 draw between two mid-table teams might not have the same excitement as a 1-1 draw between two teams at the top or bottom of the table who are close to each other in the league.

To improve the excitement of football, we should remodel the game along the lines of the American NFL. Not in terms of entertainment as a sport, because American football feels like a long drawn-out version of rugby.

The endless stoppages accommodate the advert breaks and the Superbowl itself seems to be based more around the half-time entertainment than anything else. But the example I would use from the NFL is the competitiveness of the league. No one ever dominates the NFL and every year the league has different teams competing in the Superbowl final. Between 1986 and 2006 up to twelve different teams won the NFL Superbowl and up to twenty-two teams competed in the final. No team won the Superbowl more than three times in this twenty year period. The NFL is not quite the perfect model because the league itself is saturated, as there is no relegation from the league, and no teams to get promoted from a lower division. But within the top league itself there is a high level of competition.

So why is the NFL so competitive? Simple. The teams that finish at the bottom half of the league get the pick of the best players that come through the college teams. A very socialist concept for such a capitalist society. The American Major Soccer League also employs the same draft system. Some might think that this is an incentive for teams to finish lower down in the table, but the financial rewards for finishing higher would outweigh this incentive. Some will also argue that it is a policy which rewards failure and penalises the teams who perform well. Well that's very true, which is why this particular draft system from the NFL is not the exact answer. However, what should be copied is the basic principle of giving more teams a fairer chance of competing. The culture of American football is very different to our football. The career span of an American footballer can be very short.

So the fresh players that come out from the college teams are very important as to who have the best teams in the NFL. The suggestion isn't that we give the likes of Charlton Athletic the pick of Oxford University's best players. That would just be farcical if not at least quite comical. Football (soccer) clubs have their own youth schemes and scout for their own players from the grass roots of football. If certain clubs have good scouts and good youth academies then that's commendable, and not a factor in making the league uncompetitive. In fact smaller clubs tend to have a better record of developing the best players, before they're sold off to bigger clubs. The problem of course lies in the transfer market, which is dominated by a handful of the wealthiest clubs in Europe. Here's an example of just how big the gap is. In 2007, the 20th wealthiest club in football was Benfica who declared annual revenue of £58 million. In 2001, Real Madrid spent just £10 million less than that on the signing of one player. International superstars can waste away on the subs bench because the big teams have enough resources to buy so many top players. For football to be more unpredictable then something has to be done to combat this dominance.

There is a very easy and effective way to make the overall distribution of players fairer. There should be a limit to how much one club can spend in the transfer market. A simple way to achieve this would be if UEFA imposed a spending limit of no more than €20 million euros in one season for each club – not one cent more. If a club pays €20 million euros for a player then that's their shopping over with for that season. Some might say that this idea would be unrealistic, but it's no more radical than UEFA's current transfer window law that prevents clubs from buying players throughout the majority of the season. In recent years, Chelsea have been able to outbid anyone at anytime, but a European spending limit would inevitably bring down transfer fees meaning the smaller clubs could compete more in the market.

UEFA it would seem, do view Chelsea's spending power as unhealthy for the fairness of the game and it has been reported that they hope to bring in laws to deal with it. These laws would mean that a club's spending on player wages would be based more on their annual revenue and not on the wealth of whoever owns the club. A club would not be allowed to spend crazy money on wage bills while failing to balance their books. Between 2003 and 2006 Chelsea spent £276 million on players and made losses of £228 million. UEFA have recognized that any other industry which allowed a business to operate in this way would face sanctions under competition and monopoly laws. A wage structure with a spending limit based on turnover, would stop a club like Chelsea having a complete hold on the market just because they are bankrolled by a billionaire owner with an open chequebook.

It has been claimed that the millions Chelsea spend in the transfer market is good for football because it brings money into the game. What it does however, is create an unbalanced league in which nobody else can compete. A wage structure based on turnover would also have stopped a club like Leeds United being as reckless with money as they were in the first years of the millennium. Leeds United spent way above their means, became bankrupt and then were relegated because they had to sell all their best players. A situation they found themselves in, all because one chairman overspent in the transfer market on a dream that nearly put the club out of business altogether.

There can be no doubt that the system that NFL employs makes the league more competitive and as a result more exciting. Let's compare the number of Superbowl finalists to the list of winners from the three supposed top leagues of European football over the same twenty year period:

English Premiership winners between 1986 and 2006

2006 Chelsea
2005 Chelsea
2004 Arsenal
2003 Manchester United
2002 Arsenal
2001 Manchester United
2000 Manchester United

1999 Manchester United
1998 Arsenal
1997 Manchester United
1996 Manchester United
1995 Blackburn Rovers
1994 Manchester United
1993 Manchester United
1992 Leeds United
1991 Arsenal
1990 Liverpool
1989 Arsenal
1988 Liverpool
1987 Everton
1986 Liverpool

That's just seven different winners in a twenty year period and only three different winners since 1995. Of the seven winners in this time, Everton, Blackburn and Leeds have only one title win, compared to Manchester United with eight and Arsenal with five. Hey I'm not complaining!

As a Gooner it's not my problem because I've seen my team win five league championships. I don't want the likes of Bolton or Portsmouth stepping on the toes of those of us at the top. God no, let them carry on with their annual fight for a UEFA Cup place. I would never get bored with my team winning the title every single year. But from a wider perspective, it makes for a rather boring league for everyone else. In recent years the relegation battle has provided more entertainment than the race for the title.

The 2004-05 season, was a one-horse race as Chelsea had unlimited funds and effectively bought the league championship. But on the last day of the 2004-05 season no one was watching Chelsea as they lifted the Premiership trophy. All eyes were on the relegation battle where any three of the bottom four teams would be relegated. WBA, Norwich, Crystal Palace and Southampton all had a chance of avoiding relegation, but by the end of that day only one of them would survive. It was great entertainment for the neutral fan, and was only settled in the last minute as WBA stayed up despite being the bookies' favourite to go down. Every year the relegation battle seems to come down to the wire long after the Premiership title has been settled in predictable fashion. Even the FA Cup has been dominated by a select few teams. Since 1984 to the time of writing, there has not been an FA Cup Final that has not involved at least one of these teams: Manchester United, Arsenal, Liverpool, Chelsea, Spurs.

Spanish La Liga winners between 1986 and 2006

2006 Barcelona
2005 Barcelona
2004 Valencia
2003 Real Madrid
2002 Valencia
2001 Real Madrid
2000 Deportivo La Coruna
1999 Barcelona
1998 Barcelona
1997 Real Madrid
1996 Athletico Madrid
1995 Real Madrid
1994 Barcelona
1993 Barcelona
1992 Barcelona
1991 Barcelona
1990 Real Madrid
1989 Real Madrid
1988 Real Madrid
1987 Real Madrid
1986 Real Madrid

Even less competitive than the English Premiership. Just five winners in twenty years with Barcelona and Real Madrid winning the title a whopping sixteen times between them. This sort of thing just makes life too easy for bookmakers. In the whole history of La Liga there have only been eight different league winners. The others before 1986 being Athletico Bilbao, Seville and Betis. Since the formation of the Spanish league in 1929, Barcelona and Real Madrid between them, have won forty-seven championships out of the first sixty-nine seasons. The Italian league doesn't fare too much better.

Italian Seria A winners between 1986 and 2006

2006 Title stripped from Juventus and awarded to Inter Milan
2005 Void, title stripped from Juventus
2004 A C Milan
2003 Juventus
2002 Juventus
2001 Roma
2000 Lazio
1999 AC Milan
1998 Juventus
1997 Juventus
1996 AC Milan
1995 Juventus
1994 AC Milan
1993 AC Milan
1992 AC Milan
1991 Sampadoria
1990 Napoli
1989 Inter Milan
1988 AC Milan
1987 Napoli
1986 Juventus

Seven different winners in twenty years. Juventus and AC Milan totally dominating with twelve titles between them in this time, including eleven out of the last fifteen, with the other two of that period being stripped from Juventus because of match fixing. In Seria A there have only been twelve different winners since its formation in 1929.

Scottish Premier League Winners between 1986 and 2006

I'll leave this one blank. Just fill in the year in which you think that either Rangers or Celtic won the title!

2006
2005
2004
2003
2002
2001
2000
1999
1998
1997
1996
1995
1994
1993
1992
1991
1990
1989
1988
1987
1986

The Champions League is the only major high profile league in Europe that offers any competition. Because of the knockout nature of the Champions League, the winners cannot be decided until the final game at the end of the season.

Discounting 1993, which was void (more match-fixing), there have been thirteen different winners of the nineteen Champions League finals between 1986 and 2006.

That's even more competitive than the Superbowl during the same period. There have also been twenty different finalists in this time which is just two less than the Superbowl figure of twenty-two. It's good that the Champions League is so competitive, and for that reason it is the most unpredictable league in Europe. It also provides a good excuse not to create a European Super League that the moneymen of the G14[13] have supposedly been trying to push for years and what nobody else wants (not to say that the G14 don't also adore the ultra-rich and commercial Champions League). But as great as the Champions League is from a competitive point of view, the fact remains that only a handful of top clubs throughout Europe will get the chance to compete in it. No more than four teams each for leagues in Spain, Italy and England, with fewer or no places for smaller European leagues.

The less privileged clubs will just have to carry on competing in their predictable domestic leagues. It's because the Champions League is so lucrative for the teams involved that there is such a huge gulf between those at the top and those at the bottom. When the same teams make so much money from the Champions League, they just continue to pull further away from all the other clubs. The Premiership has now got to the point where predicting who will finish in the top four has become easy. It's now considered a major achievement if a team other than Chelsea,

---

[13] The G14 are an exclusive association of eighteen football clubs: AC Milan, Ajax, Arsenal, Barcelona, Bayern Munich, Bayer Leverkusen, Borussia Dortmund, Inter Milan, Juventus, Liverpool, Lyon, Manchester United, Marseille, Paris Saint-Germain, Porto, PSV Eindhoven, Real Madrid, Valencia.

Manchester United, Arsenal or Liverpool finish in one of those top four places. This lack of competition we have now in English football is unprecedented. During the 1980s, it was a fair bet that Liverpool would win the title, but you could never predict who would finish in the next three places (indeed, teams like Ipswich Town, Watford and Southampton achieved runners-up status during this decade). The same four teams who now finish above everyone else are, not surprisingly, also the highest revenue teams in the country. If football reflects one thing in this world most starkly, then it's the wealth gap between rich and poor that grows wider with each year.

The English Premiership will never be the most entertaining league in the world until former league champions like Aston Villa, Newcastle United, Spurs and Manchester City, etc, start the season with a realistic ambition of finishing number one. At the start of the 2007-08 season, Everton were seventh favourites to win the Premiership but at 250/1.[14] In previous years, the teams who were 250/1 to win the league were the ones expected to be relegated, not regarded as the seventh best team in the country. It shows just how uncompetitive the league has become and yet it's sold as the best league in the world.

The English Football League/Premiership is the oldest in the world and dates back to 1888. Overall there have been twenty-three different league winners which is a good record and shows a very competitive history.[15] The most recent team to win the title for the first time was Nottingham Forest but that was way back in

---

[14] Odds from William Hill.

[15] The twenty-three teams who have won the English League Championship are: Preston North End (2), Everton (9), Sunderland (6), Aston Villa (7), Sheffield United (1), Liverpool (18), Sheffield Wednesday (4), Blackburn Rovers (5), Newcastle United (4), Huddersfield Town (3), Arsenal (13), Manchester United (16), WBA (1), Ipswich Town (1), Portsmouth (2), Spurs (2), Chelsea (3), Burnley(1), Wolves (3), Manchester City (2), Leeds United (3), Derby County (2), Nottingham Forest (1).

1978. The season before this, Nottingham Forest, were in the old Second Division and had no history of being a big club. Brian Clough managed Forest to promotion and within a season they were the English Division One champions. Six years earlier he achieved a similar success with Derby County who in 1972 became the twenty-second team to win the English league for the first time. This was just three years after they had been promoted from the old Second Division. The chances of any lower league club repeating this success in this day and age of football are virtually zero. Back in the 1970s, great management was enough to bring success to Derby County and Nottingham Forest. Jose Mourinho is referred to as the 'special one' and has also been described as the new Brian Clough. Like him or not, Mourinho is a very good manager whose record speaks for itself. But let's imagine that Mourinho is the manager of a fairly big lower division club that has never won the English league title.

For example Southampton FC. Could Mourinho get Southampton promoted and then win the Premiership title the following season on a limited budget? In fact, would he be able to do it in the next ten seasons? The answer, of course, is no (though Jose no doubt would claim that he could win Southampton the Champions League as well as the Superbowl). No matter how talented a manager may be, he will never win the Premiership with a club that is not in the financial hierarchy of football. Arsene Wenger is a manager who has achieved success by spending less money than his closest rivals. Although Wenger deserves great credit for this, Arsenal have still spent big money and have paid very high wages to attract top players to the club.

As we know, football is now all about making money. But if football wants to make even more money, my advice is to try and achieve a more competitive league. It certainly doesn't harm the popularity of the NFL. There can be no doubt that a more competitive league would result in a massive rise in fan attendance at matches and a huge increase in viewing figures for the TV companies. Then everyone would be happy including both the fans and the money men. I hope, one day, we will see a small club rise from nowhere to become the Premiership Champions for the first time in the club's history. It would be a shame if the number of English champions were to stay at twenty-three forever, but at the moment it looks as if it will do. Will number twenty-four please come in – your time is well overdue.

Chapter 11
A very non-commercial attitude

I'm lucky enough to have a large circle of friends who support Arsenal, and most of us live in the same London neighbourhoods such as Haringey, Islington, Hackney and Camden. The majority of us no longer attend games, and we spend a lot of time sitting in pubs and bars complaining about the commercial route football has taken, and other such rhetoric.

I know that one of our mates, called Will, got sick and tired of our continual whinging and particularly hated the phrase 'in the old days'. He became a season ticket holder at the Emirates in 2006-07, at a cost of £895 (the 'cheap seats'). What Will didn't understand was that it had taken many years of being treated with disdain from the club for me to become so cynical. It certainly didn't happen overnight. After only a short time of being a season ticket holder, Will started to feel the same way and he didn't bother to renew his season ticket for 2007-08.

He found that the club were unhelpful, arrogant and rude to deal with over the phone, and even in person. This is because they believe that they are doing you a favour by taking your money, rather than the other way round. Their attitude is that fans are easily replaceable, and if one fan disappears then business will not suffer. One night after a few pints too many, Will started to display a lot of dissatisfaction about the way the club treats the fans and made the point "*I don't think that football is that commercial. If it was commercial then it would have better customer service and customer relations. If you ask me, if it is a business then it's a very badly run business*". His point reminded me of chapter three – Customer Satisfaction. Despite the tone, it wasn't an ironic light-hearted chapter at all. I had been a club member at Arsenal for over twenty years and not once did they ever ask my opinion on anything. During this time the club had changed its whole identity, from the stadium, to the badge, to the whole corporate image of the club. After more then twenty years of support and paying thousands of pounds for the 'privilege', it would have been nice in that time to have been asked my opinion on how I felt about matters concerning the club.

Before anyone claims that it would cost a lot of money in postage to send out customer questionnaires, just bear in mind that this doesn't stop football clubs from sending merchandise leaflets and credit card offers etc on a regular basis. Football clubs never poll their supporters on their opinions which I think has always been conclusive proof that they attach no value to those opinions. In October 2007, the *Guardian* reported that Spurs might move to a new 60,000 stadium in Enfield. The article stated that Spurs chairman Daniel Levy was set to consult shareholders about the possibility of a move. However, there was no mention of Levy consulting the fans on this issue. Surely a football club with any ethics would not plan a move to a new stadium without having first got the approval from the people they hope will fill the stadium. In contrast, fan-owned clubs like AFC Wimbledon consult the fans on all important issues, including things like the design of the team kit. The Wimbledon fans are given the option of a number of different kit designs and the one which gets the most votes becomes the team kit for the following season. Most professional clubs regularly change the team kit and even the team badge, yet never consult their supporters about what they'd like to see. What kind of commercial business has no interest in what their customers think?

What had annoyed our mate Will more than anything, was a story about a friend of his who was doing a motorbike tour of Africa in order to raise money for charity. His friend, who had been a season ticket holder for fifteen years, had contacted Arsenal in writing, to ask them to donate some Arsenal stickers for his journey. His intention would be to give the stickers to kids in

Africa as a small gift. The club refused his request, even though anything that spreads the name of Arsenal would surely be good promotion for the club. Maybe to them though there is no value in promoting the name of the club to kids in the developing world who have no money to give back? What it does highlight is a distance between the clubs and the supporters, and there seems to be very little regard for the individual.

And that even applies to an individual who is loved and respected by thousands of people. In October 2007, whilst working as a bodyguard for the Pet Shop Boys, Arsenal fan Dainton Connell was killed in a car crash during a tour of Russia. Dainton, a terrace legend, had a colourful past, but by all accounts was a loveable and charismatic human being with a warm heart. Not one view heard to the opposite about the man nicknamed *The Bear*. 4,000 people attended his funeral including Ian Wight, Lee Dixon, Frank Bruno, Janet Street Porter, and the bands Pet Shop Boys and Madness. Friends and family had tried to arrange a wake at the Emirates Stadium, but they were quoted a reported £65,000 to hire out some of the facilities, which was a price far higher than expected. When the Pet Shop Boys stepped in and offered to pay for the wake, Arsenal said that it was against their policy to hold an event the day before a game, and so the wake was held in another part of North London. The club might feel that they were justified in refusing to allow a remembrance at the stadium, but by being so distant they just continue to alienate more and more fans. People were very upset about this, and the common perception has been that the club simply don't care about ordinary fans – they only care about appeasing their corporate clients. This statement from someone called Shad, is taken from *Times Online*, and it pretty much sums up the feelings that many fans have on this matter, and indeed the game in general *"It's typical of the way football is heading that the club I love shower themselves in shame in their lack of effort to accommodate the wake of a man who was widely regarded as Arsenal's biggest fan. For £65,000 I'm sure a few cleaners could tidy a room in time for a match the following day. Shame on them. Rest in Peace 'The Bear'"*. If a club like Arsenal want to profit from Shad's money, or Will's money, or my money, or the money of Dainton's 4,000 mourners, then they're going down a very unwise and non-commercial route, which will one day bite them on the arse.

One club owner who treats supporters like valued customers, is Niall Quinn, who runs Sunderland FC.[16] After an away game against Cardiff City in 2007, Quinn had heard that a plane load of Sunderland fans had been stranded at Cardiff airport, and that they would not be able to get back home until the next day. Quinn stepped in and paid for taxis to take the supporters all the way back to Sunderland. How many other club owners would bother to do that? Not many.

But by treating the fans in such a good way, Quinn is creating a culture in which he will find it easier to maintain the supporters' loyalty. If the Sunderland fans at Cardiff airport had been stranded overnight, then some of them might have started to question whether or not following their football team away from home was really worth all the hassle. However, when a club owner makes an effort to help them out of a difficult situation, he leaves behind a group of people who will continue to support them in the future.

---

[16] Niall Quinn is applying the same integrity he had as a player into how he runs a football club. He is a man who in 2002 donated all the proceeds made from his testimonial to charity (thought to be over one million pounds).

Chapter 12
Banning orders

Q: if Hollywood stars Jessica Alba and Megan Fox were to run on to the pitch during an English league game (say, Hartlepool v Macclesfield) wearing only their necklaces and campaigning for world peace would they...

(a) Get praised by the authorities for a generous display of entertainment?

(b) Win an Oscar?

(c) Get awarded the freedom of Hartlepool?

(d) Get arrested, have their names put on the hooligan register, and then banned from every league ground in the country for three years.

Answer: (d)

For English football to re-brand itself and attract a new consumer, it needed to rid itself of the stigma of hooliganism. They have achieved that aim and crowd trouble at domestic football matches has been significantly reduced in recent years – fair enough. I agree that there are people out there that do deserve to be banned from football grounds, and also from travelling abroad to follow England.

However, we are also seeing a draconian attitude being directed towards football fans, in which a person can be punished by the law and given a banning order for 'crimes' that the police wouldn't even bother responding to in any walk of life other than football. The law now goes way too far in punishing football supporters for petty acts of foolishness in the name of meeting government targets and safeguarding the corporate image of the game.

I watched England get knocked out of the 2006 World Cup by Portugal in a pub in West London. After the game had ended, about twenty-to-thirty youngsters began to throw a barrage of glass bottles at the Nandos restaurant on the other side of the street. The bottles could have injured diners and staff in the restaurant and they could have killed people who were walking in the streets. They so nearly did, as glass bottles that were thrown at length and at speed narrowly missed the heads of passers-by, including an old lady. One lad was trying to encourage people to go across the road and trash the restaurant. He was the main instigator of the trouble, but was so cowardly that he would not go over to Nandos unless more people went with him. I actually tried to reason with him, but it was like talking to a humanoid with the thinking capacity of a wild boar. I, and the people with me, could have done more to stop them, but we knew that by challenging those people it would have only ended up in a fight. Had it done so, then the police would have turned up at the right (or wrong) time, seen us fighting and that alone would have been enough to result in a banning order for football-related violence (not to mention the fact that anyone who attacks an attacker in this country is then deemed the criminal). I have no confidence in the fairness of the law when it comes to football-related disorder.

A lot of the people on the hooligan prevention list are not as dangerous as we are led to believe. A cousin of mine who follows Darlington, was considered a category C hooligan and was put on a banning order for two and a half years. His ban came to an end in August 2006 and he's now free again to attend football matches in England and Wales. I've travelled all over Europe with my cousin to watch England in places ranging from the bleakness of Warsaw and Lens, to the sunshine of Marseilles and Athens. Every time we went abroad to watch England there was always trouble, from a small scale brawl to a headline making mini-riot. Not once though did I ever see this listed hooligan actually get involved in the trouble, and yet for two and a half years he had to hand his passport over to his local police station before every England International home and away.[17] A lot of people who have been banned have been treated rather harshly, because football-related offences are not judged on an individual case by case basis. A stand-up comedian received a two and a half year banning order for running on to the pitch at White Hart Lane dressed as Osama Bin Laden! Another man from Darlington was given the same punishment for throwing a snowball at a player (couldn't they have just banned him in winter?).

At the same time more serious troublemakers go unnoticed because the anti-social behaviour they display in this country has not been football-related. Hypothetically, if I had numerous convictions for non-football-related anti-social behaviour offences and was banned from every pub in my local area, then I would not be banned from travelling abroad to watch England. Yet if I ran on to a football pitch in celebration of a goal then I would be put on the hooligan register for three years, banned from every football ground in the country and prevented from travelling abroad during England away games.

This all fits into the wider argument that football in England is now an Orwellian Big Brother environment, in which any act of spontaneous and exuberant behaviour is heavily clamped down upon. The offences that supporters get banned for in this country would be seen as laughable in other countries in Europe and South America. Football is a game of high emotion. Emotion can

---

[17] You can read an online account of my cousin's banning order, in his own words, by typing this link.

http://my.telegraph.co.uk/jamie/october_2007/football_banning_orders_fair_punish ment_or_abuse.htm sometimes lead to people acting out of character. For example a school teacher at Sunderland, who had no previous history of 'disorder', was so upset by his team's poor performances that he walked on to the pitch and chucked his season ticket placidly over his shoulder. Result: three year banning order and a fine. Yet for many more serious pre-planned crimes the police are never to be seen. Probably because they're all sitting in vans outside football grounds with nothing to do but gleam at the thought at how much overtime they're getting. Think about the police time and money that would get spent on banning just one person from attending football matches, and then compare it with the fact that the police don't have time to investigate crimes such as bike theft, bag theft, shoplifting and burglary. Why does football get this priority? Is the worst thing that can happen in our society a fight at a football match? I very much doubt that if football wasn't such big business, that there would be such high police presence for virtually every game played in this country. It's an over-enforced protection for an industry that relies on a safe and clean image to sell to its new consumers. My advice to anyone who feels a concern at the lack of police in their area is simple – just move nearer a football stadium. As for banning orders, I believe that they should be viewed with suspicion from law-abiding football fans for one very simple reason – you don't have to be convicted of a crime to receive one.

Chapter 13
Blame the pawns not the prawns…!

During the process of writing this book, one statistic in-particular has bothered me. It's made me question my own criticisms of modern football, especially when I rail against the route that football has taken since the formation of the Premier League. It's the statistic that attendances at Premiership grounds have risen by as much as 62% since 1992. Despite a small drop in attendances in recent years, 62% is a figure that can be used strongly in defence of how football has changed. I, and many others, may not like high ticket pricing, corporate priorities, players diving, music being played when a goal is scored, 24/7 fixtures, obscene player wages, overbearing advertising, aggressive stewarding etc. But as all these things and more became an accepted part of English football, the number of new fans who bought in to the Premier League went up – massively.

All I can argue then, is that popularity doesn't always make something a better product because more people buy into it. In all aspects of society popularity is not an indication of fulfilment, and in contrast the most popular things can also be the most mundane and sterile. McDonalds is the most popular food chain but I don't think there's much to be said for the quality of food they serve. There are plenty of much better burger bars where people could be happier to sit and eat, but don't. *Eastenders* is a very popular TV programme watched by millions of people, but some might say that the acting is poor and the storylines could be created by well educated gorillas. Much better programmes than *Eastenders* and *Coronation Street* will not attract the same high viewing figures. *The Sun* is the most popular daily newspaper but does it offer a better standard of reporting than *The Independent* or *The Times*? James Blunt is popular… *Scary Movie 4* is popular… Insane diets are popular... Reality TV is popular... All Bar One is popular... Capital punishment is popular... *Heat Magazine* is popular... The Chris Moyles breakfast show is popular... saying the word 'like' in every sentence is popular... wearing trousers low with your arse hanging out is popular... Adolf Hitler was popular (declared 'Man of the Year' by *Time* magazine in 1939!). Okay, point proven. Popularity doesn't impress me one little bit. In fact just to prove it a little bit more, here's a quote from Simon Cowell, a man of great taste – "I've got to tell you, if I had ten Bob Dylans in the final of American Idol, we would not be getting thirty million viewers a week. I don't believe the Dylans of this world would make American Idol a better show."

The success of the Premier League has been to convince supporters that the most important thing in football is profit. But if that's the case then why not just build an all-seated arena within the London stock exchange? We could all cheer from the stands each time one of our favourite stockbrokers sells a share. When there's so much money to be made in football it attracts people to the game whose only intention is to make a financial gain. Every other week it seems that another foreign investor is trying to take over a football club, and to put it mildly some of these people have very shady backgrounds. We're then left with a game that is run by people who are likely to put their own interests before the interests of the sport. Some will argue that football has always been about making money and to a certain extent that is true. Since the fall of the upper class amateur teams and the rise of the professionals, football clubs have been institutions with the aim to survive as well-run businesses. I've got no problem with that and I'm happy for those who work in football to make good money from the profession. But modern football has now gone far beyond just making profit and is more about obscene greed along with exploitation, and this is what is so objectionable. The debate about whether or not football has always been a business is actually irrelevant. Football may have been a business twenty years ago. It may have been a business fifty years ago. But in those times, football was not the rip-off in the way that it is today.

The big question is that would it really be a bad thing for football if the sport wasn't so profitable? When did something have to make millions and be so commercial to be of great value? Take music as a similar example. How damaging would it be to music if some record companies lost a percentage of their power as a result of internet downloading? It's perceived that if they do, then it will somehow be bad for music. It would be bad for the music industry as a profitable business, but it wouldn't necessarily be bad for music as an art form. With no big money to be made in music, then the only people involved in the industry would be the ones who actually give a damn. Need convincing? If the music industry made no profit then would Simon Cowell and Simon Fuller be working in the music industry? No. Would that be a good thing for music as a meaningful art form? Yes. No Simon Cowell and his type would inevitably mean less Westlife and their type. Do these big record labels bombard us with middle of the road mediocrity in the name of art or in the name of money?

Why should anyone really care if Virgin or EMI didn't have such a strong influence on the music industry as they currently do? To suggest that music would be harmed as well is crazy. Music has been going for as long as human beings, not as long as Warner Brothers. So when people like Sepp Blatter tell us that the World Cup would be impossible to stage without giving 31% of match tickets to sponsors, he's selling us a myth. The amount of money that is coming into football is now clearly doing the sport more harm than good. The simple truth is that no matter how much revenue comes into football, it will never be enough to satisfy the profiteers of the game, and fans of many clubs will never get a better deal in terms of ticket pricing or even ticket availability. Take for example Chelsea, a club with a billionaire owner and who have no financial hang-ups. Yet, even with all Roman

Abramovich's wealth, the ticket prices at Chelsea went higher, not lower, when he took control of the club. Chelsea maintained their status as one of the most expensive clubs in the country. If advertising money, TV revenue, and high admission prices means that a club can pay a player £60,000 a week, then it won't be long before that player starts to believe he's worth £80,000 a week. Once that player gets his £80,000 a week, he'll then start to believe that he's actually worth £100,000 a week. When that player gets his £100,000 a week, he'll look across the Atlantic to David Beckham who earns £500,000 a week, and then start to really feel like he's underpaid. In all walks of life, the greediest people are often those who have already obtained huge wealth.

So who's responsibility is it to look after the interests of the fans and make sure that the true supporters get a better deal. What about the government? At the start of the millennium the Labour Government set up the Football Task Force which was headed by MPs such as David Mellor and Tony Banks. It was set up as a watchdog to protect fans against things like high ticket pricing and commercialism. The whole project faded into oblivion which was a predictable outcome. It was never going to have any meaningful influence, because football clubs are under no obligation from the Government to do things such as lower ticket prices. All that would happen is that David Mellor and Co. would suggest to the football clubs that they should make attendance more affordable for all. The club chairman would then nod, try not to laugh and say "Okay we'll think about it!" – and then go and put up ticket prices. The owners of the football clubs must have had a good chuckle to themselves at the Football Task Force, as they knew that it was well intended but ultimately powerless. More recently in 2007, Sports Minister Richard Carbon reacted to *The Sun's* campaign to lower ticket pricing by taking the issue to Parliament. He also said that he that he would encourage the club chairmen to make the game more affordable. But with similar powers to the Football

Task Force, all any Sports Minister can do is 'encourage' and no more than that. If the Government were really concerned about fans getting a better deal, then they would bring in legislation making terracing legal once again. But this is unlikely to happen, as governments tend to prefer large groups of people to be sitting quietly, rather than take an active stand. And anyway, it's not up to the Government to help fans get fairer treatment from the sport they follow.

Football supporters need to do it for themselves. Realistically they are the only ones who can drag football out of the current culture of exploitation. What's needed is a statement that sends a powerful message to the people who run the game. A statement not necessarily in words but one that would humiliate those who have taken advantage of us in recent years. As someone who has grown up a football fanatic, my weekends have been built around going to watch my team play.

Whatever game you go to you always hope for a big crowd. Football fans want to be part of a sell-out crowd and never like to see thousands of empty spaces in the stadium. However, now there should be a desire to see empty football grounds all over the country. It would deliver a powerful message if thousands of fans stayed at home, or better still, stood outside the stadium on match day instead of sitting down inside the ground. It would send a shockwave through football and would change the way the game is run overnight.

Many people believe this would never be possible and that the current state of football is irreversible. The same way as people dislike the way that global corporations dominate the world, but don't feel that there's anything they can do to change things. Tony Benn warned (in the documentary film *Sicko*) that an effective tactic in controlling people is by demoralising them – make the masses give up hope which then leads to apathy. My suggestion of boycotting matches will be counteracted by the argument that if fans of clubs like Liverpool, Arsenal, Manchester United, Chelsea,

Tottenham and Newcastle United boycotted games, then thousands of others are lying in wait to take their place. There is no doubt truth in this, but football like everything else is not invincible, and can rise and fall at any time. Football is a now a business, therefore it can come unstuck if it makes too many bad business decisions. Once there is a stigma attached to being a fan who is part of the problem, then things would start to change. The current breed of consumer who have taken over football do so partly out of trend and status (with the exception of a lot of younger fans who never had the chance to stand on a terrace). Where were these supporters in years gone by? Most of them are old enough to have been attending football for decades, and yet it would seem that they have only been attending football for a very short period. People like myself and thousands of others who kept the game going in years gone by have been away from football for too long now, and I think it's time for us to return. For us to be able to, we need the help of those true fans who have kept loyal to their football clubs throughout this time.

At a club like Arsenal many of the fans in the stadium are genuine true supporters and have been for years. Going by the conversations I have had with a lot of these people they are fed up with the way the club treats them, but they don't feel that there's anything they can do about it. If they did temporarily boycott football then it's true that others would take their place – but not enough to fill a 60,000 stadium week in and week out. A boycott taken by all true fans might only leave 10,000 empty seats in a 60,000 stadium, but that would still be a huge statement. Those 10,000 empty seats would represent the fact that something which was once exclusive, no longer is.

The mercenaries and trend followers will not want to be part of something that is rejected by thousands of others, and a small gesture is one that can trigger a much bigger one over a period of time.

Fans who want to make some form of protest should boycott games and that's a tough thing to have to do, but what other option is there that would have any effective outcome? Peaceful protest doesn't usually get anywhere. Violent protest is usually counter-productive. The only protest that will ever work is an economic protest that hits the pockets of those at the top. Hypothetically, if Britain and America were to invade Syria, then there could be six million people on the streets of London and Washington in protest against an invasion – but it wouldn't change a thing. The only thing that would stop them would be a people's boycott of the big corporations that fund politics. Corporations such as the American supermarket giant Wal-Mart (Asda in Britain). If Asda shoppers, opposed to an invasion, boycotted Asda then Wal-Mart would lose a lot of revenue. Wal-Mart lobbyists then put pressure on the White House and threaten to withdraw financial backing for political campaigning if the invasion goes ahead. It is only at this point that the politicians take notice of the argument against war. Since 2007, football supporters have started to wake up to the problem of ticket pricing. Campaigns and petitions have started to be launched by supporters' groups aimed at reducing the cost of football. It's all wasted energy though – simply stop going to matches and we will start to see a reduction in cost that fits in with the prices of the other European leagues. Otherwise the best we can hope for will be petty 10% reductions on season tickets, or a freeze on prices for just a season.

Staying away is the only way for fans to get a fair deal for themselves and retain their dignity, instead of just being pawns in making others filthy rich. English fans have to prove that they can stand up for themselves, because in other countries it's the strength and community amongst the supporters that has maintained fairness in the way they are treated. Italian and German fans simply stopped going to football matches when they started to feel that they were being ripped off. In fact, German fans went so far as to have picket lines outside the stadiums. Their tactic worked and that's why a ticket for any top game in these countries can be bought for as little as €10 euros.

Writing to a club in protest at ticket prices will not make much difference if the person who writes the letter continues to pay £40 a game every other week. Football responds to simple market forces, which is why ultimately it is the fans and not the clubs who deserve the most blame for the way that football is run. If a grocery store sold apples at £15 each and people still bought the apples, then the grocer would be an idiot to change things.

Thousands of fans all over the country are keenly waiting for that economic downfall in football whilst continuing to keep the gravy train moving. If they are waiting in hope for the people who run football clubs to gain a conscience then they will be waiting a very long time, because their attitude is callous and one-dimensional. Football clubs are run like global corporations and their sole aim is to make as big a profit as they can legally get away with. They don't understand the concept of 'How much is enough?' The big question for football fans is whether or not they are happy with the way that football is run. Deep down do fans feel satisfied with the product that is being sold to them, and do they feel dignified being customers in this market?

For the fans who feel totally at ease with the way they are treated, I wish them all the best in what they have. If this is the case for the vast majority of football fans then I'll give all the credit in the world to the people who run the game in bringing such a sense of fulfilment and belonging to so many others. I'll just be left with a belief that being economically superior doesn't make a community any happier if they judge absolutely everything in terms of making more money. The four most prosperous countries in the world are USA, Japan, Germany and Britain. Part of this wealth is built on long working hours and a culture based on consumerism. But who will stand up and honestly claim that, that wealth alone gives those of us in these countries a better or more meaningful way of life compared to those in places like Sweden, Canada, New Zealand, Malta, Fiji, Norway, Iceland, Jamaica, Trinidad etc? In a BBC poll in 2006, over half the people surveyed believed that Britain was a worse place to live than it was twenty years ago. Even though in 2006 Britain had less crime and was economically stronger than it was in 1986. In 2006 only 29% believed that other people were trustworthy compared to 44% in 1986, and 60% in 1950. Another poll in 2006 from the company Filofax revealed that two thirds of people would accept a lower wage if it meant having more time to themselves. So much then for money bringing happiness!

Football nowadays is economically better off than it was in 1986 or 1950, but we're not happier and we certainly don't trust the people who run the game.

Chapter 14
The light that never goes out...

"The only thing necessary for the triumph of evil is for good people to do nothing"

Edmund Burke

Okay, okay, I know that's a little over the top. We're talking football here not repression and murder. This Edmund Burke quote is one that is usually associated with millions of people in concentration camps and ethnic genocide. But the general principle of this quote is that for wrong 'uns to get away with doing bad things, it takes other people to let them get away with it.

In 2005, American tycoon Malcolm Glazer took control of Manchester United. Many of the United fans were very upset, about this, mainly because Glazer had to borrow the money in order to become the overall shareholder. Their argument was that this would put the club into debt, which would inevitably lead to a large rise in ticket pricing. The first two years went by without any admission rises, however by 2007 the club did indeed raise ticket prices by 12%. As a result of this take-over, fans from Manchester once again had a club which they could truly feel part of. It is a club where the fans have genuine power and a say, and where the owner's priority is in the interest of football and not financial profit. I'm not talking about Manchester United, don't be silly. I'm talking about FC United Manchester. A new football club founded in the year 2005, who play their games at the stadium of Bury FC. After the Glazer takeover, a strong group of disillusioned Manchester United fans didn't go along with the belief that if you can't beat them, join them. FC United's first ever season was in the North West Counties Football League Division 2, which they got promoted from in 2005-06. A season later in 2006-07, they won promotion from the North West Counties Division 1, and at the time of writing they are four divisions below the Football League.

When I first heard about the plans of these United fans and their splinter club, I thought that it was nothing more than an over-ambitious project unlikely to enjoy even short-term success.

Yet having watched a television documentary on this new football club, I believe that FC United could have a longer and more interesting impact on English football than anyone thought possible. Just a year after their formation, they had established a fan base of 4,000 supporters who are prepared to watch FC United in small northern divisions, against teams who can't even pull in 100 fans. The 4,000 fans they are capable of attracting is already more than nearby established league clubs such as Rochdale, Bury and Stockport County. If this amateur club can pull in 4,000 fans in such a low division, then what would happen if FC United actually made it into the Football League? The thought of them achieving league status in the future is by no means unrealistic. Every time FC United get promoted to a higher league, more fans will take them seriously, and if they ever reach the division below the Football League then a regular fan base of 10,000 could very well be achievable. The culture within FC United is a reminder of what football has lost and what football could once again be in the future; if all true supporters reject the greed and commercialism that has been imposed on us. FC United's fans stand up throughout the whole game and appear to make more noise than the 75,000 at Old Trafford do at most home games. There looks to be a great community feel at the club and a sense of enjoyment that is so lacking elsewhere in football. As one female fan on this TV documentary simply puts it "When football becomes all about money, it's no fun is it?" At FC United there is genuine democracy and all the supporters have a say on off the field matters, in a similar way that the fans of Barcelona and Real Madrid do. FC United are an industrial and provident society. This means that they do have shares obtained though membership, but they can be bought for as little as £1, and all members have the same amount of power regardless of how many shares they have. FC United have a manifesto that includes the following principles:

1. The board will be democratically elected by its members.
2. Decisions taken by the membership will be decided on a one member one vote basis.
3. The club will develop strong links with the community and strive to be accessible to all. Discriminating against no one.
4. The club will endeavour to make admission prices as affordable as possible, to as wide a constituency as possible.
5. The club will encourage young local participation – playing and supporting – whenever possible.
6. The board will strive as much as possible to avoid outright commercialism.
7. The club will be a non-profit organisation.

The owners of FC United are not empty-headed dreamers with an unrealistic ideology. They come across as intelligent and passionate people who should not be underestimated. The seven principles of this manifesto are all ideals that thousands of football fans everywhere will embrace. These are principles that should be the basis of the way all football clubs are run, especially principle number seven that states that the club will be a non-profit organisation. A football club should operate on the basis to financially survive, but also to look after the people that support them, and to serve the community.

FC United are certainly not the first of a kind and are not unique. Other clubs in England that are owned by the fans themselves include Brentford, Notts County and Stockport County. Arguably the most high profile is the amateur club AFC Wimbledon, who are a splinter club of the old Wimbledon FC, the club who now go by the name of Milton Keynes Dons FC. The old Wimbledon FC were a club that many football fans all over the country had a soft spot for, because they were a small fish surviving in a big pond and they caused a stir along the way. Milton Keynes Dons on the other hand are a club which fans all over the country disrespect because of the way in which the owners took away a football club from one community and gave it to another. Fans all over England view the Milton Keynes Dons as a false club with no history or credibility and they were branded 'Franchise FC'.

Very much in the same way as people look at Milton Keynes the city. No one dislikes the fans of the Milton Keynes Dons because they're just supporting their team and are no different to the rest of us. The disrespect lies with the directors and owners who in 2003 quite literally took Wimbledon FC about fifty miles away from one city to another. It was all the brainchild of music entrepreneur and promoter of Milton Keynes, Pete Winkelman, who is now the chairman of the Milton Keynes Dons. He was keen on the idea of Milton Keynes having a high profile football team and had tried and failed to get other struggling clubs such as Barnet, QPR and Luton Town to move to the city. The directors of Wimbledon FC were prepared to make the move, much to the overwhelming disapproval of the fans. In the 1990s the same fans had feared that their club was going to be moved all the way over the Irish Sea to Dublin. Wimbledon were a Premiership team at the time and because of this I'm sure that the 'Dublin Dons' would have attracted massive crowds at Lansdowne Road. It was a novel and exciting idea for football fans in both England and Ireland. As an Arsenal fan I would have loved to have gone to watch my team play a Premiership match in Ireland. But it didn't happen and that was the right decision. The basic principle as to why the move would have been wrong was that the most important people in the debate were the established fans of Wimbledon FC, who were happy with their club being in South London. The relocation of their club to Milton Keynes was finally confirmed in 2002, a year before the change was actually scheduled to take place. In Wimbledon's last ever season in South London, the fans returned the favour of rejection and boycotted the matches resulting in the club going into administration. Their home fan base had fallen to just triple figures while their away support went no higher than double figures. The fan base of the Milton Keynes Dons is similar to that of the old Wimbledon FC and averages around the 5,000 mark. The dream for the Milton Keynes Dons is that they will one day attract bigger crowds and rival the big city teams in England.

If Pete Winkelman and Milton Keynes were so desperate for a football team then they should have done what every other professional club had to do at the beginning of their history. That would be to start at the bottom and make their way up to professional status. The irony is that if there was one team in the country who achieved this rise to the top in such a short period of time, then it was the old Wimbledon FC. They went from non-league football to the top division in just ten years. They were the hope and example for all small clubs in the country. Now their memory represents a fear that all small clubs can justifiably have. The fear that a businessman can take a football club away from a town or city by using small crowds as an excuse, and then relocate in another part of the country.

This franchising is another Americanism that we simply don't want in our game. We have no desire to see our football clubs relocated to other cities through the desire of the owners and not the fans. The city of Los Angeles has been without an NFL team since the Los Angeles Raiders became the Oakland Raiders. The

Oakland Raiders claim the history of the Los Angeles Raiders. In fact they could move to the other side of the country, become the Cape Cod Raiders and still claim the history of the Los Angeles Raiders. From 2003 until 2007, Milton Keynes Dons claimed the history of Wimbledon FC. Therefore in the Milton Keynes Dons honours list they credited themselves as FA cup winners from the year 1988. The famous final when underdogs Wimbledon beat mighty Liverpool 1-0. This claim on another club's history was without merit, and eventually the trophies and medals were sent home to Merton council in South London.

AFC Wimbledon unofficially claim the history of Wimbledon FC. On their website they have released the following statement in justification of them doing so – *"The supporters of AFC Wimbledon believe that our club is a continuation of the spirit which formed Wimbledon Old Centrals in 1889 and kept Wimbledon Football Club alive until May 2002. We consider that a football club is not simply the legal entity which controls it, but that is a community formed by the fans and players working towards a common goal. We therefore reproduce the honours won by what we believe was, and always will be, 'our' club, in our community."* There can be no doubt that AFC Wimbledon is the same club as Wimbledon FC. They have the same club colours and symbols, more importantly the same fans, and in case anyone forgot they're called Wimbledon. The franchise team from Milton Keynes was never the same club from its very formation. The team colours and symbols are different, the fans are different and in case anyone forgot, they're called Milton Keynes Dons.

In effect all they did was to take Wimbledon's place in the Football League while the real Wimbledon FC was taken over by the fans, had a slight name change by one letter, and ended up four divisions below the Football League. But despite the injustice, AFC Wimbledon could one day rise above the Milton Keynes Dons, who at the time of writing have suffered two relegations. AFC Wimbledon have realistic ambitions to one day rise again to the Football League and if they do, it would be a great victory for the Wimbledon fans and a great slap in the face for the so-called entrepreneurs of football.

What could be unique about FC United is that they have the most realistic opportunity of causing a bigger stir within the game. Manchester United will always be a global super-club and be well supported no matter what FC United ever achieve. But if FC United ever do make it to league status, then a sizable minority of Manchester United fans could very well start to support them instead. They would not be abandoning Manchester United, they would simply be rejecting the money driven culture of the Premiership which is not the same thing.

FC United fans carry Manchester United symbols to the games and they also sing Manchester United songs. A true Manchester United fan can feel as at home at FC United as he or she would inside Old Trafford these days. A friend of mine complained that the fans of FC United are timewasters and that they should have just gone off and supported other local teams such as Stockport and Bury instead. What would be the point in that though?

Those other local clubs are to put it simply, other clubs, and nothing to do with disillusioned supporters of Manchester United. The whole point of setting up FC United is that they are a splinter club where the owners and fans believe that a forgotten spirit of Manchester United lives on. Of course, the downside is the standard of football that is played. No one can deny that it would be tough to go from watching the skill of Wayne Rooney to watching a bunch of amateurs. However, if FC United do continue to rise, then the standard of football will improve with each year. Maybe FC United will go in the other direction and fade into oblivion as I initially thought they would. Just maybe though, FC United Manchester will one day in the future play Manchester United in a competitive game. Imagine that? If it were to happen, then it would be a great victory for true football fans, and serve as a warning to clubs all over the country who treat their fans so badly.

I've concentrated a lot of this book on blaming other fans themselves for the commercialism and greed within the sport. But as a supporter, what have I really done other than stop giving financial backing to the money men of football. Those involved in FC United and AFC Wimbledon have gone so far as to take positive action and create something that they do believe in, rather than just moan and reject something which they don't agree with. Some may not see the idea of fans turning their back on a club as very positive. But the most negative thing us football fans can do is sit back and do nothing. AFC Wimbledon and FC United appear to have both integrity and ambition, which puts them a class above those whose only ambition is money. They prove that the spirit and soul of football really does live on, and I hope they can do more than just survive, and that they can achieve that priceless longevity. So then, just in case this is the future, anyone up for creating Cannons FC? or Villains FC? or AFC Liverpool? or Blades United? or AFC Everton? or Newcastle City?

Sources

History of Football, DVD – Freemantle Media.

Totally Bill Hicks, DVD – Channel 4.

The Rules of Association Football, 1863. Bodleian Library.

Brian Clough, Cloughie: walking on water – my life. Headline Book Publishing.

Ashley Cole, My defence. Headline Book Publishing.

Evening Standard. Daily Mail. Daily Mirror. The Daily Telegraph. The Guardian . The Independent The London Lite. The London Paper. The Metro. The Sun. The Times. USA Today.

BBC News and Sport.

bbc.co.uk.

Fox News.

BBC Panorama 2006.

Tax Rate Information Centre.

Wikipedia.

Powerslam (magazine).

Sport (magazine).

Time (magazine).

Deloitte.

Football Fans Census website.

The Football Network.Net.

TALKsport.

Official websites for all Premiership clubs up to the 2007-08 season.

Official club websites for Leyton Orient FC, Millwall FC, Milton Keynes Dons FC, Oakland Raiders, FC United Manchester and AFC Wimbledon.